My
Wild Ride
on a
Carousel

(By the Caterer Who Couldn't Cook)

Bill Jones

BALBOA.PRESS

A DIVISION OF HAY HOUSE

Balboa Press books may be ordered through booksellers or by contacting:

Balboa Press
A Division of Hay House
1663 Liberty Drive
Bloomington, IN 47403
www.balboapress.com
1 (877) 407-4847

Because of the dynamic nature of the Internet, any web addresses or links contained in this book may have changed since publication and may no longer be valid. The views expressed in this work are solely those of the author and do not necessarily reflect the views of the publisher, and the publisher hereby disclaims any responsibility for them.

The author of this book does not dispense medical advice or prescribe the use of any technique as a form of treatment for physical, emotional, or medical problems without the advice of a physician, either directly or indirectly. The intent of the author is only to offer information of a general nature to help you in your quest for emotional and spiritual well-being. In the event you use any of the information in this book for yourself, which is your constitutional right, the author and the publisher assume no responsibility for your actions.

Any people depicted in stock imagery provided by Getty Images are models, and such images are being used for illustrative purposes only. Certain stock imagery © Getty Images.

Print information available on the last page.

ISBN: 978-1-9822-5172-7 (sc)
ISBN: 978-1-9822-5173-4 (hc)
ISBN: 978-1-9822-5174-1 (e)

Library of Congress Control Number: 2020913696

Balboa Press rev. date: 07/31/2020

If one advances confidently in the direction of his dreams, and endeavors to live the life which he has imagined, he will meet with a success unexpected in common hours.

—Henry David Thoreau

Contents

MENUS

Getting Started

I have been asked many times, one way or another, "How did you get involved with the catering business?" This was followed by questions like "Was your father a chef? Did your family own restaurants?" My answer was that my father was not a chef. He was in prison for fifteen years during my childhood. None of my five siblings or I knew where my father was. We were told he was in a hospital in upstate New York and had a blood disease.

My mom would go to visit him monthly. Sometimes, if she could afford the cost, one of us would tag along. Being the youngest, I remembered little about my father. I was only four years old when he left to serve his sentence. It has never been spoken of, but I am sure my older brothers knew where he was. So to answer the question, my dad was not a chef, and we did not own a restaurant. We were a family of eight, counting my parents, and we were on home relief or, as some call it, welfare. This meant we were broke, in scramble mode to survive, and dependent on that monthly aid check.

Despite this, I did not have a bad childhood. In fact, it was very interesting. There was a lot of activity in our house, and my mom did whatever she had to do to keep us all together. There were times when she was afraid we would all be put into foster care. She constantly had to think of ways to raise extra cash; some were legal and some not so much.

One day, I remember a policeman came to our door and gave my mom a coupon for a free Easter basket that contained food from neighborhood food stores. It included condensed milk, canned vegetables, and other nonperishable items. We went down to the police station with our coupon and retrieved our basket. On the way home, she was very quiet, which meant she was planning something.

I looked at her, and she said, "This is what we're going to do. Next year, you're going to volunteer to help fill the baskets. But every time you put one item in the baskets, you put two items in a basket under the table, which you're going to sneak home."

I was scared stiff and tried to explain to her that I would be *at the police station*, and what if I get caught? Her answer was "You're too young and skinny. No one will even be looking at you. They'll be too busy." So the next year rolled around, and I did what she asked. At the end of the day, I had so much food in my hidden basket that I could hardly lift it. But she was right. I struggled out with my basket, and no one said a word. It may be that they saw me and knew that we really needed that food. If that was so, I'm grateful to them.

My mom was not a highly educated woman. I don't think she finished high school. But she was very street-smart. And her devotion to her family, and even to my father, was unbreakable One day she decided that we had to have more money from the state, so she told me she was going to show them how thin and sickly I was. Hopefully, this would convince them that she needed more money. She instructed me that at the interview, when she tapped my foot, I should fall on the floor as if I had fainted. Well, I did it! And we netted an extra ten dollars per month for the effort.

My mom also liked to entertain to keep us happy. So each Thursday, she would gather all the kids on the living room floor and perform Broadway shows for us—ones that were currently on Broadway and others from the past. I still carry some of those old tunes in my head. One that seems to appear on occasion is called "Maisy Dotes," and another one is a real tearjerker called "My Mother's Eyes." You could say we were poor but happy.

Uncle Willie

I n our building, there were many small apartments. All the tenants were friendly and stayed out of each other's business.

Every once in a while, we would come home, and in front of our apartment door would be a bag of groceries containing items like cereal, canned goods, bread, and jelly. I would ask my mother where they were coming from, and she would say, "They're from Uncle Willie."

"Who's Uncle Willie?" I asked.

She replied, "He lives at the end of the hallway. He's a nice man. Now mind your business, and if you ever see him in the hallway or anywhere, do not speak to him. *Do you understand?*" She always knew I was nosy.

Though I was curious, I did what I was told. It turned out that Uncle Willie did not live in that apartment. Some older lady lived there, and he would bring her groceries too. I saw him going in and out once or twice, but I obeyed my mother and never said a word to him.

One morning going to the store, I passed a newspaper stand, and on the front page was a picture of Uncle Willie. He had just been arrested for bank robbery. His name was Willie Sutton.

Needless to say, that was the end of the grocery deliveries. But I never forgot his generosity and try to emulate that every chance I get.

Gran Mal

I was looking forward to finishing high school, and I loved learning different things and reading about adventures and people and just having a good time.

One day I was watching a sandlot softball game in my neighborhood, when I experienced my first grand mal seizure. It was very scary, but that was just the beginning. I experienced more and more each day, until I began to feel that I no longer had control over my life.

After one of us hurt ourselves, my mom would often say, "It's only growing pains!"

After waking up from my first epileptic seizure, she said the same thing. But it wasn't growing pains, and they continued at the rate of up to eight seizures per day. At that point, my mom was asked by the superintendent of schools to take me out of school because I was scaring some of the students.

It was a scary time for me too. Once a confident kid full of laughs and joy, I now found myself frightened and unsure of my future. After a period of feeling sorry for myself, I finally got off my butt and decided that I wouldn't let this hold me down. I started to look for a job by day and get my GED by night. It didn't occur to me that because I was taken out of school due to the seizures, no one would hire me.

Undeterred, I would get up every morning and look at help-wanted ads in the *Brooklyn Daily News*. I would circle certain ads that I liked and head out for the day in search of a job. In my first three weeks, I had many seizures, and I also had many jobs—the longest lasting eight minutes, or until the next seizure.

During that time, I would head to the job on my list, fill out an application, and sometimes not finish due to a seizure. And that was that, so off to the next job application. What I remember as being funny, in a masochistic kind of way, was that on all the job applications there was a question asking, "Do you have fainting spells?" And I would think, *They must be kidding! If they want someone with fainting spells, they have found their man!*

I tried to get a job making lamps, being a shoe salesman, and the trying went on and on.

One day I had circled six of the ads, and there was a job for a kitchen helper to a caterer. It had been a very weird day, having seizures and banging or bruising something on my body a few times. I was starting to get frustrated, and I must have looked a total mess, but I was down to the last circle. I crossed my fingers as I went to the address of John Larsen Catering.

I remember that my head was hurting and my nose was bruised. Some sight I must have presented myself. I was frustrated and pissed off about all these failures, so when I arrived at his door and John introduced himself, I blurted out, "I want a job! I will do the work of two guys! I have fits, but if you hire me, you can't fire me because of that."

I never knew exactly why, but hire me he did. Maybe he felt sorry for me. Maybe it was like *My Fair Lady* in that he saw a poor kid from the streets and thought he could make something of me. Who knows? But at last I had a job and perhaps someone who believed in me.

John was known for his liver pâté, which he sold to many gourmet shops and high-end hotels throughout New York City. He put me up on a wooden Pepsi Cola box in front of a large vat of goose liver and told me to stir the goose liver with a large, wooden paddle to get it ready for baking.

I was excited, and I really wanted to please him. He was the first person to show belief in me, so I stirred and stirred, and before I knew it, I had a fit and fell into the vat. John heard the splash and called an ambulance. I was rushed to Doctors Hospital. He was there upon my awakening. I worked for him for almost six years.

So the reasons I began my career in the food business were epilepsy and luck of the draw.

John Larsen

ohn catered cast parties for show openings on Broadway as well as the cream of the crop socialites in New York City, many celebrities, the Catholic archdiocese of New York, and others. He made a great impression on me and somehow saw something in me that made me want to succeed.

He was very protective of me early on. One example I remember is when we were catering a party at a fancy apartment on the Upper East Side and he was behind the buffet while carving the meat. I started to have a seizure and literally crawled under the table, where he would nonchalantly rest his foot on my chest so I wouldn't roll out from under the table. Meanwhile, he'd keep carving away as if nothing was happening.

John was a big man born in Denmark with a heart as big as his body. He certainly changed my life, and because of my association with him, I was able to meet with and dine with some of my favorite Broadway and motion picture stars.

John was married to Swedish film actress Signa Hasso, and she had many friends in show business to whom we catered, such as columnist and writer Walter Kerr *(Please Don't Eat the Daisies)*, pianist Victor Borge, and comedienne and actress Hermione Gingold, to name a few.

After about two years working with and learning John's method of catering, I was beginning to feel good about myself and my future, even though the seizures were still an issue. I knew that I had a father figure in my life and someone from whom I could not only learn but who trusted me in decision-making.

The next couple of years were like magic. I was meeting so many interesting people and working alongside my mentor, but as they say, the holiday was about to end. My mom, at the age of forty-seven, died of a heart attack. My dad was now out of prison and at home and was not very pleasant. I remember how just a few months before he came home, my mom changed from performing musicals for us to a game that involved drawing a magical line in the corner of the living room. One of us would be put behind that line. From there, you could say nothing while the rest could say anything or do anything except touch you. One day after watching my dad be really mean to my mom, I asked, "Why is he like this?"

She reminded me of the days when I was told to stand behind the line and had to take all the taunting and verbal abuse from the rest of the family. "Well," she said, "you did that for fifteen minutes. Your father did it for fifteen years. Some men come home better, and some come home bitter."

John stayed with me through these family traumas, including my mother's death, and was very supportive. He kept me busy with work after the funeral was over to take my mind off it.

Alec Guinness

John was a master chef and a wonderful culinary arts specialist but a terrible businessman. Some of his clients often mistook his kindness for weakness by saying (lying) after a dinner party that they would recommend him to a dear friend and then clear up the bill—and many never did. When we were through serving a small dinner party and presented the invoice for the food and labor, they would suggest that they would call John in the morning and take care of the invoice then and send the staff home without even a tip.

Knowing so many people in the show business community and having the opportunity to meet them was a big boost to my confidence, and I started acting as John's business manager of sorts. If John didn't get paid, neither did we staff members, so I began to tell those clients that we had to be paid up front, which did not sit well with John or some of our clients.

One was an old dowager whose son lived with her and was somehow in show business and had many dinner parties for top-name stars. When I made it clear to her that we now required upfront payment, she became very unpleasant toward me, not because she had no money but because I had the gall to tell her how to entertain. She made it clear that I was just the server and did not give orders except to the staff, and I should never address guests unless they required something.

She was a very memorable lady, although odd. For example, she always insisted that she open the door when guests arrived. If she was talking to a guest and the doorbell rang, she would pull that guest to the door and greet whoever was there. One evening she was speaking with Fay Wray and the doorbell rang, so she dragged Fay to the door. It was Edward Everett Horton. She said to Edward, "This is Fay Wray."

Edward's response was "Fay Wray? I thought we were both dead!"

The dinner guests on this evening included Ms. Wray, Mr. Horton, the hostess, her son, other celebrities, and the guest of honor, Mr. Alec Guinness.

During dinner, I could feel her eyes on me as I served her guests. Somewhere before the main course and dessert, she said to Mr. Guinness, "Alec, look at this young man with such tattered clothes. You must have many suits that would fit him." I wanted to jump over the table and choke her, but instead I went on serving. I guess I could say we had a love-hate relationship, and I was also very young at the time.

The next morning, I was called up to the front desk of our hotel. Waiting for me there was a linen suit bag with three beautiful, tailor-made suits, and attached was a note saying, "Keep Your Head High. Alec Guinness." I was of course very surprised and excited. The suits were made in England of a nice woven tweed that had cuffs on the sleeves, which I had never seen.

From then on, I was looking good, if I say so myself. I never forgot that incredible act of kindness and generosity. It says a lot about who Alec Guinness was beyond the famous acting career.

Another one of those memorable ladies was Elsa Maxwell, the dame of etiquette. Ms. Maxwell, which was the way one had to address her, was a well-known social party planner of small events that always received favorable reviews in local society magazines.

She was very stern on how all serving personnel were attired, and we always had to have pressed shirts and shoes shined. She was not very tolerant of facial hair on those who were serving, and we were instructed to stand straight in front of our assigned tables and always smile as guests arrived (something I found myself always demanding from staff members when I started my own company).

One of Ms. Maxwell's clients was Helena Rubenstein, the distinguished cosmetics entrepreneur, major art collector, and philanthropist. She had a beautiful brownstone on the east side of New York City and was expecting about thirty guests for dinner. Ms. Rubenstein had been in Europe for a while and had just arrived home the night before.

As usual, Ms. Maxwell called on us to arrive long before the scheduled arrival time of the guests so that she could be absolutely sure the centerpieces were perfect and the help met her expectations as far as dress code. When all was well, we stood at attention in front of our assigned tables, ready for review, and smiled. Ms. Rubenstein came by to take a look and was, I think, very pleased at what she saw.

Well, we all stood there smiling, it seemed, for almost thirty-five minutes. After some frantic discussions between Ms. Maxwell and Ms. Rubenstein, it was decided that there would be no dinner after all because there would be no guests. Apparently, someone—thank God it wasn't me—had forgotten to send out invitations.

As they say, "Shit happens." And the catering business is no exception.

Ms. Maxwell was also responsible for the grand opening of a yacht club on Long Island. The plan was that guests would arrive and have wine and champagne served in the clubhouse and then lunch served on a pier overlooking the water. Ms. Maxwell was there being as fastidious as ever, and this being her first grand opening, she was snapping her fingers, letting all know what she wanted and to make sure that everything was ready when the guests arrived. Tables were set to her approval, and as a light wind wafted in from the ocean, all that was left was to fill and ice the water glasses.

As we headed for the water and ice, I looked up and noticed the pier was sinking! So there was no need to fill the water glasses. Tables, chairs, linens, glassware, silverware, and flowers were floating in the ocean or had sunk to the bottom.

In the end, we improvised and all the high-society guests sat on benches provided by the yacht club. They ate box lunches we bought from a local delicatessen.

If I was taught anything from my New York experience, it was to never give up. I didn't make much money, but I was able to learn about the human experience more than I could ever learn in any school.

John, as I said, was much respected and most people thought he was very well off. But I knew different, as there were times when we couldn't even pay the utilities. Yet he stayed strong and always told me to "know that all always works out." I have taken those words with me during the most difficult times of my life.

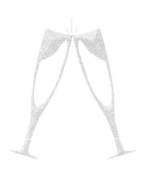

Table Manners

After a few years, John got an offer to take over food service for a hotel on Park Avenue, and we were providing room service and lunch as well as the hotel bar.

One day, John told me that a friend of his was coming from Europe and we were going to host him, his wife, and some of their friends for dinner. When I was told who was on the guest list, my jaw dropped. His friends were Lars Schmidt and Ingrid Bergman, and their invited guests were Marilyn Monroe and her escort, Hermione Gingold, and the host, of course, John. He wanted me to oversee the table setting of fine china, flowers, and candles and to be sure all servers wore clean uniforms. I would act as "captain."

I complained, saying that being so close to his operation, I should be part of the dinner, not captain of the staff. He responded by telling me that I had the worst table manners he had ever seen and that was the only reason I couldn't join the dinner. I was heartbroken and think I even cried, so he said he would be willing to teach me table etiquette for one week, and if he was not satisfied, there would be no more pleading. I agreed.

I don't know how, but I passed the table manners test and got to sit at the table with the guests. When the evening of the event came and all the guests arrived, I was introduced to each as John's assistant, and it made me feel good although a bit nervous. I asked the captain to bring me tiny pieces of whatever I ordered so that it would be easy to eat and I would not do anything to embarrass John.

I sat very nervously at that table between Marilyn Monroe and Ingrid Bergman, both looking beautiful in expensive, tailored suit jackets and blouses. I watched as Lars Schmidt slurped his soup and Marilyn smoked at the table. The language by others was appalling, and I couldn't wait to let John know about his friend's table manners. His response was "I know that, but they were not representing me and you were—and you were very good."

As I said, John was from Denmark and for a while was married to Swedish actress Signa Hasso. Their marriage ended after a few years due to her movie commitments in Europe, but he later married a beautiful model and they had a daughter. That marriage didn't last either, but many years after I had moved to California, I got a call from John's ex-wife, who wanted me to cater her daughter's wedding. As the saying goes, "Every cloud has a silver lining." You just have to be patient enough.

California, Here I Come

I had now been with John for almost six years and was getting a little tired of doing parties. I wanted to do something different. The fits were still coming, and now that my dad had returned home from prison, things got a little crazy in my house. As I mentioned, that's when my mom died from a massive heart attack. And on top of all this, I was tired of hiding the fact that I was a gay man.

We lived in a neighborhood that was Italian, Irish, and Jewish, and I thought that if word got out that I was gay, it would be an embarrassment to my siblings and my father would kill me. I remembered my mom's advice: "Trust your father, he just needs time." I was beginning to come out as a gay man and had a bad encounter with another guy. I was hurt badly so I went to my father, hoping for some love and support. Instead, what I got was a fist in the face and the admonition to get away from him and the family. So much for paternal love and understanding.

So I bought a one-way bus ticket to California.

At the depot, I went to the little coffee shop and bought my last dinner in New York, thinking about all the wonderful food that John had prepared and some of the incredible kitchens where I had eaten those foods. Now there I was at a bus terminal and eating a hamburger while remembering John's quote: "Know that all always works out."

After paying for the bus ticket as well as the hamburger, I bought Hershey bars to eat during the trip across the country. I wound up with $1.47 in my pocket.

The bus was very nice, although the trip took six days and five nights. That's a lot of Hershey bars. The trip was not memorable, except for a lady who sat across from me. She watched me take out one of the Hershey bars and eat half a bar for lunch and a full bar for dinner as other guests went to the restaurants at each stop.

When we arrived in Albuquerque, New Mexico, this lady asked me to please carry her bag and escort her to the restaurant. I didn't know why, but figured I had nothing better to do. I took her to her table and immediately smelled the aroma of freshly baked bread. I sat her down and started back to the bus when she tugged at my shirt and asked if she could buy me a bowl of soup. I'm not a great soup lover, but the aroma was so great I thought, *Why not?* Along with that bowl of vegetable soup, I ate an entire loaf of bread and a quarter-pound stick of butter.

That dear lady and I never saw each other again, but I did promise her that when I got settled, I would write and give her my address – and I did. One day about a year later, I received a package with a gold-plated Hershey bar and a gold pair of lips. She claimed that she told the Hershey Company about this young man who only ate Hershey bars across the country and always had a pleasant smile, and they had sent this to her. I can't verify that to be true, but it was a sweet thought on her part and amazing that she would remember me at all.

It must have been 15 years later when my aunt told me that my father was dying and wanted to see me. My domestic partner, Steven, suggested that we send my father a round trip ticket to LA. We did and when he came out, he and I buried the past and began a six-month friendship before he passed away.

Lesson learned: Mom was right again, all he needed was time.

California, Here I Am

As you can see, I came to California not because I had aspirations of being in show business but because I was broke and felt it was better being broke in warm weather than in cold.

Looking through an old newspaper I found at the bus terminal in downtown LA, I saw a nice little hotel called the Cine Lodge that offered a single room, indoor swimming pool, continental breakfast, and potluck dinner for twenty-five dollars per week.

Besides the $1.47 in cash in my pocket, I also had a check from Chase Manhattan Bank, but unfortunately, that account was closed. Undeterred and figuring I would make it right somehow, I took the room and gave the manager the bad check. My life in California had begun. (Know that all always works out.)

As it turned out, most residents did work around the hotel to help pay their rent. That worked great for me, as I had no job yet. And I loved the potluck dinners, including hearing all the stories from residents who were either in show business or wanted to be.

Bob Lieberman

I was able to find a job at a well-known catering company ten minutes on the bus from my new home. I stayed for almost two years at the Cine Lodge without paying rent, as I was the person who vacuumed and changed the linens in all the rooms, starting at 6:00 a.m. I was not very popular with the late risers.

This company, Casserole Catering, was like John's except that it catered larger events. And as John was the finest chef I had ever seen, my new boss was the best salesman I had ever known. His ability to come up with ideas for an event in a matter of minutes always astonished me.

After approximately one year, we became very close, for he loved the business and so did I. He allowed me to start selling for the company. And it was there that I met the Beatles, the Monkees, Elizabeth Taylor, Elvis Presley, the Rolling Stones, David Bowie, Della Reese, and many more.

Among some of the large events that Casserole catered were movie premieres, which were held under beautifully adorned tents that seated thousands and were usually decorated in the theme of the particular film the studio was promoting. So Bob, the incredible salesman, would usually get the job if there were bids required.

Bob would call me late at night just to talk about ideas he had, and I would give him my ideas. He had a son who was going to law school and now I understand is a very prominent attorney, but his son had little interest in the catering business.

Among the things I learned from Bob Lieberman was "Always say yes, and then find a way to get it done."

The Beatles

I believe the year was 1963. Bob Lieberman got the job of taking care of the Beatles. It was their first tour in California, and we had to find a location where they could live while they were there. The agency representing the Beatles wanted to put them up in an estate in Beverly Hills, but it had to be secluded and have at least eight bedrooms and a soundproof room for them to rehearse. An estate was secured and rented for one month at an enormous cost. Every time they came back to California, a different estate had to be leased for security reasons.

I remember going back to the Beatles' house one afternoon and driving up to the gates when I was surrounded by hundreds of girls screaming for the Beatles. There was security at the gate so that no one could enter, but as I drove through the gate, a girl threw through the window of my car a paper bag containing a letter to John and a pair of her panties. Being stunned for a moment, I crashed into a palm tree and wrecked the driver's side of my new Camaro.

Lesson learned: with the Beatles, proceed with caution.

My coworker Roy King along, with a chef and a server, had free access to the house so it was only a few times I personally interacted with any of the Beatles, except George. He invited me to play a game of pool. Apparently, he played pool a lot in his hometown, and so did I. I found George to be the warmest of all the group. If they weren't so well-known worldwide, they would be regular young guys in Liverpool.

The rest of the group was always pleasant to me when I was at the house, although I found the people who traveled with the Beatles were far more difficult and demanding. I also found different purveyors around town who took advantage. If told something was ordered for the Beatles, prices skyrocketed. For example, there was a store in Los Angeles where I used to buy tailor-made shirts. Someone recommended that the owner make a few shirts for one of the Beatles. I was privy to the invoice, and just let me say that with what this guy charged for that shirt, you could have gone to the Caribbean for one week.

But the guys were also a bit extravagant. One time for dinner, they sent our chef to Mexico for authentic Mexican food.

After the issues with the crowds and ingress at that first house, this became one of our main concerns. However, no matter how careful we were, we discovered that fans will do stupid things to be close to them. One day in the Hollywood Hills house they had rented, I walked out to the pool area, which had a seventy-five-foot waterfall cascading down to the swimming pool. Something made me look up, and I saw a girl carrying a small baby standing on a very slippery slope above the pool. I called the police, and she was saved from her own folly. I learned that for some people, all reason goes out the window when passion is involved.

I enjoyed every bit of my time with the Beatles and feel lucky to have known them.

Carousel or Casserole?

W e catered large movie premiere parties like *Camelot, Chitty Chitty Bang Bang,* the revival of *Gone with the Wind,* and too many more to remember. The cost of catering these studio events became very expensive for us, and due to the fact that it was done to benefit a charity, it became difficult to justify the expenses. So eventually these events went to hotels where tents were not needed, as well as all tables, chairs, linens, china, cutlery, and other necessities, so more money could be given to the specific charity.

Approaching my sixth year at Casserole and learning more about this business than I ever thought possible, we were informed that the owner, Bob Lieberman, had sold the business, which at that time was named to a holding company in New York.

I started to inform some of my clients—CBS, ABC, and KTLA—as well as corporate accounts about the sale, but I was always asked the same question: was I getting cash or stock? I had no idea what they were talking about so I decided to speak to Bob and was told that I would keep my job but that was all.

After thinking about it for some time, I, along with a coworker, gave our resignations and decided to start our own company. Thanks to most of our past clients who always mistakenly introduced me as Bill Jones of "Carousel Catering," not "Casserole," that's what we named it. As I answered in a lawsuit years later claiming a similarity in names, I explained that a carousel was a merry-go-round and a casserole was a dish.

I won.

After we left to open Carousel, most of the clients moved with us. They included Milton and Ruth Berle, Mr. and Mrs. Gregory Peck, Jeannie and Dean Martin, Johnny and Joanna Carson, Sammy Davis Jr. and his wife, John Wayne and his wife, Mr. and Mrs. Norman Lear, Jimmy and Cluny Komack, and many more who remained our clients for years. In fact, we catered for the Carsons, the Martins, the Waynes, the Lears, and the Komacks for several different events.

Stepping Out on Our Own

My partner, Roy King, and I were fairly well-known in the industry, and we opened our doors relying on his knowledge of weddings and other social events and my clients in the entertainment industry as well as corporations.

The day we signed the corporate papers, we had no money, no kitchen, and no trucks. We used to cater a lot of events at one of the temples when we were at our former place of employment, so a deal was made to trade services for use of their kitchen.

Eventually we found a former hair salon in Burbank, which became our first office, and we were on our way.

Our first catering jobs were for small events, such as bar mitzvahs, weddings, cocktail parties, and parties for celebrities like Della Reese *(Touched by an Angel)*.

We were asked to cater her wedding to her manager Franklin and then years later Della's daughter's wedding, both held at her home on the top of Bel Air Drive in Bel Air,

California. They had an indoor swimming pool, and Della liked to have the pool filled with gardenias. Sometimes, the pool being filled with the aroma of that many flowers made it difficult to breathe.

Many times I regretted having made such a bold move starting from nothing. But here I am fifty years later. I'd say it turned out pretty well.

What Happened to the Wedding Cake

Roy was a joyful guy but also what I like to call a pat man, meaning that he had special ways of doing things and if there were any changes to what he had planned, he would get all flustered.

One of our first jobs was a wedding at a local temple in Hollywood, and as suggested, they delivered on time and placed things exactly where Roy wanted them placed. The only thing they neglected to tell him or me was that they made a brand-new cake table but it was slightly wider than usual. Roy worked in the kitchen setting up food service, and I worked on the floor as a captain.

So on this occasion, I did my job on the floor and Roy sent out each course from the kitchen as planned. The wedding cake was delivered by the baker, and as Roy was finished with food service, he began decorating the cake table, which was approximately four feet long on and casters. When Roy got done with his decorations and flambé, it was beautiful.

It was always planned that when Roy heard the band leader start "Here Comes the Bride," he would roll the flaming table out across the banquet hall to a place where the cake-cutting ceremony would take place. This evening, after dinner was served and tables were cleared of any debris, I gave the orchestra leader the okay to start the music. As the music played, I looked toward the kitchen, but there was no Roy. At first, I thought maybe he was not quite finished with his decor.

The leader played a second chorus—still no Roy.

I rushed to the kitchen, which meant that there now was no cake, no captain, and now no Roy. I found Roy almost in tears trying to force the cake table through the narrow door. That little extra width just wouldn't fit, so I suggested that we go out the kitchen door onto the street and wheel this flaming wedding cake a half a block and deliver it in the front door. That all worked fine, except the mothers of the bride and groom were in the kitchen looking for us and were starting to panic.

But we finally entered the front door of the banquet hall with Roy pushing this flaming cake table and perspiring, and I swear his tux was shrinking. Little did we know that due to all the wheeling on the rough street, the locks on the legs of the table had opened. As the crowd was giving a large round of applause, and Roy triumphantly wheeled the table across the slick wooden floor, the cake table collapsed.

A shriek went up from the crowd and echoed across the room.

The cake, thank God, was on a wooden platter and the table was covered in a silky material. So the cake slid on to the shiny floor across the hall almost back to the kitchen. The cake was not damaged and never touched the floor, but we all had to scramble to put out the flames.

After a few weeks, we were invited to dinner with the parents of the bride and they were very generous with nice comments. We all had a good laugh.

The Largest Catering Event in History

Six months later, while sitting in our little three-room Burbank office and reading the *LA Times*, I came across a story stating that a new shopping plaza was being built in San Diego, California, and a grand opening was planned to benefit the Children's Hospital. The anticipated guest count was to be twenty-five thousand!

The anchor stores like Broadway, Bullock's, and others paid all costs for the evening, so ticket sales were given to the charity. Guests paid twenty-five dollars for food, drinks, and entertainment. The entertainment for the evening was Ms. Peggy Lee, Herb Alpert and the Tijuana Brass, and the Mickey Finn band.

Roy was convinced that I had lost my mind for even considering bidding! We knew nothing about an event of this size, such as how much food to order and the number of staff. But I figured we had no houses, no money, and no serious bank accounts, so what could they take from us if we blew it?

So remembering the words of my former boss, "Always say yes, and then find a way to get it done," we bid for the opening.

About two weeks later, the meeting planner called saying how pleased she was with our proposal and that she was bringing all the reps from the anchor stores to meet with us at our facility on Monday. Now even I started to sweat as we had no kitchen facilities and no trucks, and of course, Roy started to panic, saying that they would send us out of town on a rail. He suggested that we drop our bid. I suggested that we give it a little thought.

I went outside and right across the driveway was a well-known restaurant named Sorrentino's. I knew they had a banquet room so a plan started forming in my mind. I went over to see George, the owner, and persuaded him to let us use his banquet room as a front for the big meeting and agreed that in return, he could provide all alcoholic beverages and share in bar revenue.

But Roy was still not happy, pointing out that there was no Carousel Catering, only Sorrentino's. We had about $400 in the bank, and I used every penny of it to rent twelve panel trucks. I found a person who made stick-on magnet signs reading, "Carousel Catering," with the phone number, and plastered those on the vans, and we were ready.

When the meeting planner and all the bigwigs arrived, they saw all the vans outside Sorrentino's, the big banquet hall, and somehow we pulled off the illusion. The meeting went very well. They signed our proposal and gave us a check for $20,000, and the planning began.

With the down payment, we provided 247 buffet stations, ninety-six bars, and six hundred floor personnel from wherever we could get them. Gas stations, shoe stores, restaurants, and of course staffing agencies. Each buffet was fully self-contained with all the food. And in total, enough food to feed the country of Bangladesh! For example, we served something like 650,000 hot and cold hors d'oeuvres!

We had seventy-two chefs working seventy-two hours straight in rotating shifts in tents provided by and on the shopping center. We had a very successful event, although we ended up making almost no money. It was said to have been the largest catering event of its kind ever performed. And most importantly, it put us on the map.

We were tired but happy that we pulled it off. While cleaning up all the mess, including about 250,000 cocktail napkins, two guys came to me very drunk and asked if I could show them where the restrooms were, and I did. One guy saw Herb Alpert and went for an autograph while the other drunk guy went to the Port-a-Potty. Unfortunately he stepped in just before the truck hauling the trailer with the Port-a-Potties pulled out. Apparently, he sat down in San Diego and wound up still asleep on the toilet in Santa Ana.

We received some notoriety for planning this event, and one of my TV interviews before the event was on *The Joey Bishop Show*. Joey wanted to have us on his show and provide a mockup of one of our crudités displays, but Joey was not so pleasant. He wanted to just make a joke of it and made it clear that he did not believe that we could set up so many stations. At one point, he picked up a black olive from the table and asked me, "How many olives will you be using, Mr. Jones?" I was so mad I blurted out, "350,000," and he looked aghast. I thought, *I lied on TV, but who will count the olives?*

Some months later, I received a call from a rep of an olive company in Italy who wanted to give us all the olives we needed for the event. And all they wanted was a mention with a card on each station. Those olives lasted for ten years.

After getting so much press from local television, radio, and newspapers, Carousel, Inc. was starting to be looked at as a serious catering service and we began getting calls from representatives of Motown, Elizabeth Taylor, David Bowie, Diana Ross, Michael Jackson, and many more.

Catering across the Nation

C arousel was the only caterer that traveled across the country from city to city, bringing along all the food from Southern California. And the company received a lot of notoriety for that. The one exception on the menu was certain dishes for which the local cities were known. One example was peaches in Georgia, for which the state is famous (although I found out later that the peaches were smaller there than in California). But mum's the word on that in Georgia.

The peach deal happened when my local produce man in LA told me of his brother in-law who had a similar produce operation near Atlanta, and he could deliver to me rather than taking the produce from California. So I called this guy. He was very pleasant and told me that he could do the job. I gave the date that I needed everything and the order, and he said that it would be done.

The day of the delivery to the Fox Theater in Atlanta, he arrived on time with everything for which I'd asked: five cases of grapes, pineapple, oranges and eight cases of peaches and other produce. When I looked at the peaches,

I almost screamed as the peaches in Georgia were the size of baseballs and in California, they were the size of softballs. Steven had to go to every supermarket in Atlanta and buy all we could to make up the difference. Apparently, the supermarkets in Atlanta were also enamored of the California variety. Size matters!

Surprise!

One of our favorite clients for whom we catered many events, such as bar mitzvahs, bat mitzvahs, social events, and weddings, was a sweet couple named Sally and John. They had a beautiful home in the San Fernando Valley with a tennis court, on which all events took place. Sally and John worked for Sally's father, who owned a clothing company that manufactured very nice sweaters for men and women. The business was very successful and Mama and Papa, as Sally's parents were called, were semiretired and in their eighties.

Every year, besides the charity events and long after the bar and bat mitzvahs, the family always had a birthday for Mama and Papa. Working with Sally was a joy for me because not only did she like to spend money, she was into themes for parties, with each a little over the top from the last. Once they had a huge circus theme with clowns, live animals, magicians, and of course all under the big top tent on the tennis court. Then there was a Moroccan theme, a "Rhapsody in Blue" theme, and on and on.

The one that stays in my mind is the last one ever done at Sally and John's beautiful home and the last time we catered for them. Again it was the birthday for Mama, who I think was in her late eighties. The theme was to be Raggedy Ann and Andy.

I was immediately impressed and ready to cater this event because I had never seen this theme used. Sally, of course, was coordinating all the props and colors, arranging for all the costumes, and going half out of her mind with the stress. She had it planned that all the husbands would wear Andy costumes and all the wives would wear Raggedy Ann costumes. As she explained, Raggedy Ann was more important than Andy, so she wanted me to wear Raggedy Ann and the staff to all be Andys. Well, I hadn't come out yet as being gay, and now it was all going to come out as a girl doll! I convinced her that the staff should remain as normal.

On the day of the event, I was setting up the tennis court decor when Sally's daughter said that her mother wanted me to open the door when Mama and Papa arrived. I didn't understand, so she went on to say that this was a surprise party; Mama's real birthday was two days away.

I hated surprise parties, and I'll tell you why. I was about to celebrate one of my birthdays but some time before had met this handsome man in Hollywood. I tried to get to know him better by bribing him with lunch, dinner, or drinks, but nothing ever worked. We were in the same social circle, but that didn't matter. I was batting zero.

Until I got a call from him asking if I would like to do dinner and a movie in a couple of days. I thought, *Finally I'm getting somewhere.* So we went to dinner in West Hollywood and I was ready for the movie, planning maybe later *Humm!* But he surprised me by asking if we could skip the movie and go to my house. I really needed to go to the men's room, but I wasn't going to let this guy get away. So I hurried off with him.

All the way driving over Laurel Canyon I had to pee but figured I would as soon as I arrived home. Well, we arrived, I opened the door, and thirty people screamed, "Happy birthday!" I stood there in front of my dream boy and thirty other friends and wet my pants.

So I told Sally's daughter that I wouldn't open the door for Mama. I figured if a young man could pee when someone yelled surprise, who knows what could happen to an old lady? Luckily, another family member took over the door-opening task and I was off that hook.

The time finally came, the guests were all gathered, the doorbell rang, and the scream of "Happy birthday!" came roaring across the room. Mama immediately collapsed and was rushed to the hospital.

I was left with the unenviable task of presenting the invoice to Sally, and I did so as humbly as I could under the circumstances. But we needed to pay our staff.

That was a hard one.

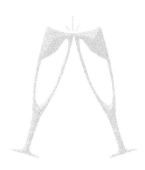

For the Birds

Like many young businessmen, it is standard to try to do all that is asked of you from a client and more. There was one mother of the bride who hired Carousel to do her daughter's wedding for about two hundred guests. It was mid-December in LA, a little chilly but clear as a bell. It was in a temple in the San Fernando Valley. My client claimed she was recently in Bavaria and witnessed "a magical" wedding take place. She said that as the wedding couple left the church, a man let doves fly overhead, and she wanted to know if we could do that for her daughter's wedding.

I explained that the dinner would be inside at the temple hall, not in the Bavarian countryside. She asked me to please try, and try we did. We found a man called the Birdman of Burbank. He had a little shop in the valley from which he sold a variety of birds like parrots, parakeets, and more. He kept his homing pigeons in big cages in the back. Those were the ones he had trained for a long time. When I told him my client's desire, he suggested we take a look at the venue and see if it could be done. He then explained that he only had pigeons, not doves. They looked the same to me and that was good enough at this point. Anything that could fly and looked like a bird would work.

We arrived at the temple to scout the location, and after a few minutes, the Birdman of Burbank claimed he was sure it could be done. The florist built a long cage over the wedding party's table and covered it with ferns and other florals. There was a perch long enough to hold twelve birds, with two velvet cords attached to a false bottom that were to be pulled by two very handsome waiters to release the pigeons. Then according to the script, they were supposed to fly around the room, astonishing all. At the sound of a whistle from the Birdman, the pigeons were to return to the cage.

Well, during the afternoon, we did a few dress rehearsals, and the birds were perfect. It was amazing to see. We launched into final preparations for the event.

Alas, unbeknownst to any, especially the Birdman of Burbank, the florist had in the interim placed the cage over a heater. So when the magic moment came during the dinner and the waiters pulled the cords to a wonderful drum roll, twelve dead birds fell on the wedding party. The mother of the bride went hysterical, and it went downhill from there.

The Birdman was a gentle person, but as I see it, we all lost something: he the pigeons, the client her beautiful wedding, and Carousel the client. As I presented her final invoice, I knew I would never hear from her again. I didn't.

"Be Sure You Get What You Asked For"

(Another Mother of the Bride Story)

It was a day in June just in the rolling hills above the Pacific Ocean in Malibu, California, the sun shining brightly a gentle breeze—beautiful.

I had worked for this couple since their daughter was a teenager, so years later, I was asked to cater their daughter's wedding. Three weeks before the wedding, the mother and father took a brief vacation to Hawaii. When she returned, she told me about an orchid drop at a wedding, which is customary on any Hawaiian island.

She reminded me that her husband, Joe (let's call him that), loved roses and asked if we could drop the petals at the wedding as a surprise for the wedding party, but for Joe as well. I don't know the true facts, but the gossip was that Joe was a mob boss of some kind and whenever he attended a party where there was a live band, the band had to know and he had to sing "The Days of Wine and Roses."

Knowing that this was planned for the wedding, my client asked if I could arrange to have rose petals dropped while Joe was singing. So I contacted a helicopter service from Van Nuys and connected them with a floral company. I got both to coordinate the drop and all looked good—that is, until I got exactly what I asked for.

As I said, the day was beautiful. Maybe a little windy. The wedding was going great, the band was playing, and I could see Joe heading for the stage. And that of course meant we all were about to hear "The Days of Wine and Roses."

I signaled to the man on the ground with his walkie-talkie, and he immediately informed the pilot to bring up "the bird." (That's what he said.) Over the horizon, I watched as the helicopter got closer and closer, and the first breeze from the whirling blades ruffled the tablecloths. A few moments later, the tablecloths were fluttering like crazy and the surprised, to say the least, guests looked up at the chopper.

I heard the man with the radio tell the pilot to make the drop, and out of the sky fell twenty-five huge bags of rose petals.

Unfortunately, no one had told the pilot to open the bags, and they dropped like bombs on the terrified ensemble. Guests dove for cover or ran for their cars. I think Joe dropped the mike and ducked under the stage. Not such a good look for the "mob boss."

Another tough invoice to deliver. I guess he really wasn't a mob boss, or it could have been curtains for me.

Doctors of Pepper

A month later, Steven and I went to Las Vegas to search for a location that would be interesting and could accommodate a large group for Dr. Pepper. I knew that the University of Las Vegas was a culinary arts school, so after looking at other places like the ranch owned by Wayne Newton, we went to the kitchen manager of the university and asked him for advice. He suggested a building on campus that was within walking distance from the kitchen.

We decided to take that walk and were amazed at what we came upon. It was a typical college building that housed the pool for swimming practice. But what was amazing about this building was that it had a forty-foot-wide staircase that led to the roof. Up there was a planter that I could see with a little imagination would be a perfect stage for Linda Ronstadt and the Nelson Riddle Orchestra. On each side of the planter/stage was enough room for one hundred tables and chairs as well as buffets for dinner.

I called my contact in Dallas and told her about this incredible building. She expressed her excitement, and shortly after, she, along with executives from Dr. Pepper, came to meet with me at the site. As I explained my ideas for the event, I could see the excitement in their faces and was sure I had the job.

We were all supposed to meet for dinner that night, but Judy walked in alone—not good. I asked what was wrong, and she told me after thinking it over, her boss felt it was not up to Dr. Pepper's standards to take these very important bottlers out of a beautiful ballroom to a roof top.

I was disappointed because I thought I had the job, but then I had another idea. I asked her if there was a real Dr. Pepper. She laughed and told me no. The wheels were turning, and I said, "How about each of the bottlers get a certificate of graduation from UNLV as doctors of pepper? She loved it, and the job was ours.

We usually hired a trio during cocktails, but I felt that this was special place so I hired the UNLV Chorus to sing all Dr. Pepper jingles as cocktails were passed. This was done on the first floor, and when the dinner was to be served, we had thirty white-tied and tailed violinists, fifteen on each side, come down the staircase while playing "Rhapsody in Blue." As the guests started up, each staircase would light up.

Dinner was received graciously and went without a hitch. Linda Ronstadt was almost finished with her show when all of a sudden, the biggest sandstorm in one hundred years hit Las Vegas. Eight hundred guests ran for cover. It was a wild scene, but Linda stayed and said to the audience she would finish the show if they would stay, and they did.

Another Airport, Another Plane

C arousel had catered many events in other cities since that Dr. Pepper sandstorm in Las Vegas. In fact, the majority of our business was catered out of town.

To me, a party was a party no matter where it was. It simply took a few meetings and coordination of all the necessary details, and we would pack what we needed and head out, sometimes by truck and sometimes by plane.

I remember getting a call from a catalytic converter company that was planning a VIP dinner to be held in San Antonio for one hundred guests. We showed her the facilities we thought she would like, and she chose the McNay Art Museum. All was looking good.

However, when I arrived home from San Antonio, there was a message on my phone from another meeting planner (for Toshiba). They had an event planned for one thousand guests, but it was scheduled to be held in Atlanta the day after the San Antonio party. And we had already booked another event in Philadelphia two days after that. This seemed like an impossible schedule, but there was no way I was going to turn down an event for one thousand people. So of course, I accepted.

I did not know how to tell this to our executive chef, David Erickson. I thought he was going to strangle me, but he stood by me as always and produced three incredible events, but not without some unforeseen circumstances.

It was decided that we would split up and I would go to Texas with my group, my partner, Steven, would go to Atlanta with his group, and then we would all meet in Philadelphia for the final event. We would ship all food and kitchen items on different planes, and each group would go to their city to begin prep work.

My food arrived right on schedule, but Steven called and said he had been waiting all day in Atlanta and so far, no delivery. Panic struck. We were on the phone for almost two days, only to find out that the plane never left Los Angeles due to an electrical failure, but the airline guaranteed the food would arrive the very next day. Now we were two days behind, and that really put the pressure on.

But because I had such an amazing staff, all three events went off smoothly. From that moment on, I always prayed that David and his staff never quit because I would be up the creek without a paddle.

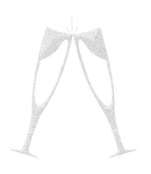

They Do the Work—
I Get the Glory

O ne year, the Dr. Pepper Bottlers convention was scheduled for Maui, the planning was underway, and soon so would be the staff. There were times when I was a little full of myself and took so much for granted regarding my staff, who did all the work, while I got the glory. Here is an example.

Steven and I went to Maui and spent ten days looking for locations that could host over two thousand guests, including a name entertainer. We met the meeting planner and showed her the sites, and we finally settled on the Maui Tropical Plantation located on the Lahaina side of the island. We were awarded the contract and given a sizable down payment. So we left for the mainland planning to come back to make the final arrangements. But there was trouble ahead.

In the past, we simply went from city to city renting kitchen space from local caterers or used workspace in the venues where the events took place. However, not on Maui.

Apparently the meeting planner spoke to the banquet manager of the hotel where they were staying to arrange for us to use that kitchen for the event. However, she was told that the kitchen could not accommodate that large a group. Apparently, because I was with a catering company from the mainland, I was a "persona non grata." No way were they going to help me.

I wasn't aware of any of this until I arrived back on Maui. So I had already used up the deposit money and had no kitchen for my staff to make this event happen. I had to get back to LA to try to figure what the next step would be.

Upon returning to our facility in Palm Springs and getting the staff together, I just felt somehow it would be all right and the answer would come. First, we started to plan lodging for the staff, which turned out to be twenty condos at a complex in Lahaina. It was right next to the ocean and a nice place for the staff to kick back after a hard day. I also thought twenty condos meant twenty small kitchens—the answer to our kitchen dilemma! But that idea was overridden quickly by saner minds, and I agreed.

I had asked Chef David to do his magic so many times, like when he had to poach a salmon in a woman's dishwasher or thaw one hundred pounds of shrimp in a bathtub. But no amount of magic was going to make the twenty-kitchen idea work. We had to find a big kitchen, so off we went to Maui for another trip.

Steven and I were eating a meal on the plane, and another light went off in my head. I asked the flight attendant where they cooked this food. He told me it was prepared by a company called Dobbs and that they provided food on most of the airlines. He went on to tell me where their kitchens were located on Maui and that they were at all airports across the country.

So as soon as the plane landed on Maui, we went directly to the Dobbs kitchen at the airport. I spoke to the general manager, who told me to call their corporate headquarters in Canada. After a brief conversation followed by what seemed like a mountain of contracts, we had found our kitchen for Maui and for other cities in the United States with the Dobbs airport service.

Four years later, I was having dinner with the executive with whom I had spoken on Maui and asked why he let Carousel use their space. He replied that after our event, he noticed an upgrade of productivity in their kitchen. He claimed that it was the way his staff was treated by Carousel. That worked for me.

We now had a kitchen to use that was probably ten times the size of our kitchen. We had the location, and we had condos. We were set. Until we were told there were not enough tables, chairs, linens, china, or cutlery on the entire island so they had to be shipped by boat at a huge cost to the client. But that's what we did. There were no options.

It turned out to be a super affair. The client was happy, I was happy, and the staff got an extra seven days to relax and enjoy the beach on Maui.

Maui Stories

I don't know why, but it seems like we were working on Maui a lot. One example was a dinner for Smith Barney for one hundred guests. We rented the home of country-western singer Randy Travis. It was very charming with gold records on all the walls as well as photos of famous people in the entertainment business and others. It had a nice garden that faced Front Street and the Pacific Ocean and was about twenty minutes from the Ritz Carlton Hotel in Kapalua.

During the event, guests mingled throughout the home while enjoying hors d'oeuvres and cocktails followed by dinner in the garden. And just to add a little more excitement, Hurricane Niki blasted the whole island and the winds were so incredibly strong that roads were closed in and out of Maui.

But as they say, it was a good party up till then.

Clients were beginning to call Carousel due to referrals or from being contacted by one of our sales staff. One such client was Smith Barney, who engaged Carousel to cater a VIP client and sales personnel event for six hundred guests four nights in a row. It was held on the grounds near the La Quinta Hotel in Palm Desert, California. The meeting planner was so pleased that the following year, she asked us to find a place on Maui for a special meeting that was expected not to exceed one hundred guests.

Shortly after, we were asked to find an interesting location for an event for *PC Magazine.* This one was to be held on the opposite side of the island in Wailea, so we started to look for a place that would meet their needs—and searching we did. After what seemed like days asking local residents for possible locations, we were getting nowhere.

One day Steven was reading a real estate magazine that featured unique homes on Maui. He saw one that was very beautiful, but there was no address and no phone number. However, it did name the area in which the home was located. It was called Wailea Heights.

Off we went to search for this house, and after driving up and down different streets, we finally found it. I remember Steven asking, "How are we going to get in to see it?" I replied, "Ring the bell!"

The gate was secured with monitor and voice system, and a male voice asked what we wanted. After I explained, he opened the gate and let us come up to the house. It was magnificent! The lower level had a beautiful swimming pool that contained fish that were able to somehow swim with people and tolerate the necessary chemicals to keep the water safe.

On the way up to the living room, dining room, and bedroom was a painting studio. The owners were Peter and Lynn Tucker, and we all became fast friends and brought other clients to them over the years. I purchased one of Lynn's paintings, and they came to visit Steven and me in our home in Palm Springs.

Other locations available on Maui included the Willie Nelson Home and many more. The golf course, where a seated dinner for Chrysler was accomplished, was located very close to the Ritz Carlton Maui.

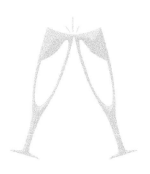

The Super Bowl

A local Palm Springs meeting planner called me to tell me she had a potential large Super Bowl event for a prominent auto manufacturer for 750 dealership owners and their wives. They wanted a continental breakfast, followed by a light lunch and snacks. They also requested Bloody Marys and mimosas. Plus they wanted a gourmet dinner served in the evening with a full bar. That sounded good so far. Then she said that it was to all be on board Amtrak train cars going from Indio to Union Station.

Could we do it?

I remembered those words from my old boss saying, "Always say yes, and then find a way to get it done." I discussed it with Steven and Chef David, and they agreed it could work, so I said yes.

A few weeks later, we all met at the Amtrak train yard to start planning how to execute this task. First, we found out that there were no kitchen facilities available, and there were fifteen train cars that sat forty guests plus a number of smaller private train cars owned by individual train enthusiasts providing seating for the rest.

The dish-up area was on the platform between each train car, and on that platform was a transit box for the hot food and a cooler for the salad, dressing, and dessert, with a small table for salad plates. In that space was also enough china, cutlery, glassware, and napkins to serve that car as well as the staff.

On the day of the game, our staff had to leave Los Angeles around 2:30 a.m. to get to Indio in time to load all food and beverages on board. The rental company loaded all rentals on time as well, and we were ready. Early that morning, guests were taken from Palm Desert by buses to a railroad station in Indio for the two-and-a-half-hour ride to Los Angeles and the Rose Bowl. After the train ride, we served a nice continental breakfast and snacks.

All guests enjoyed this light breakfast as well as the specially designed box lunch that David provided, but they really loved the Bloody Marys. We pulled into Union Station and all guests were then bused to the Rose Bowl.

And then after the game, we were to meet the guests on the platform of Union Station in downtown LA for the ride back to Indio. While the guests enjoyed the game, our staff started loading all necessary supplies for the dinner on the way back: food, beverages, china, cutlery, glassware, and cooking equipment.

The Rose Bowl game was over around 6 p.m., the guests arrived at Union Station around 6:30, and thirty minutes later, we were on our way back to the desert. The guests obviously enjoyed themselves as they were smiling and some even singing. I thought they were either a real nice crowd or they'd had a good party at the Rose Bowl.

As soon as it was possible, the bars were open and drinks were served, and as requested, we started dinner service to a really happy crowd. The first course was a wedge of lettuce drizzled with David's great Caesar dressing, followed by filet mignon with a Bordelaise sauce, and that was followed with a trio of desserts. Everybody was happy and devoured their food.

We were warned that chartered passenger trains had to stop for trains passing in the opposite direction, and sure enough, we were stopped for about forty-five minutes to let a freight train go by. Now that happy group was getting a little testy, asking things like "What the f___ is happening?"

Then the train started to move again and did so for about another hour, and then it stopped again. This time, it was not for a train passing but because there was a dead body on the tracks and we had to wait until the body was removed. One could understand why this crowd was a little anxious as they were probably up for fourteen or fifteen hours, but there was nothing the Carousel staff could do as David tried to explain to one woman, who took out her anxiety by slapping him across his face so hard his knees buckled.

We were only thirty minutes from Indio and everybody was tired, including the Carousel staff, but as usual, they did the job expected of them and went above and beyond. A few weeks later, we received a letter from the meeting planner saying how much they enjoyed themselves, and I guess that's all that matters.

Lesson learned: When quoting a cost, especially for labor, don't estimate it only for the event itself. I assumed ten hours for each staff, and in the end, they all worked almost twenty-four hours after returning to our facility in Los Angeles.

I think Carousel is the only company to have catered a gourmet dinner for 750 guests onboard a moving Amtrak train.

Memorable Things That Happened at Catered Affairs

There was an organization that raised money to plant trees in Israel. These events gathered about four hundred to five hundred guests and were typically held in the garden of a beautiful home in Beverly Hills or the surrounding area.

The concept was to select a man or woman celebrity and honor them with a Crystal Award that was in the shape of an obelisk and nice words would be said about the individuals and their kindness to that charity. Many notables from show business had been awarded this honor over the years.

This time, the award was given to three people: Jimmy Stewart, Mae West, and Glenn Ford. This particular year, unfortunately, the event happened during the Six-Day War between Israel and Egypt and all guests were in an understandably somber mood. Jimmy Stewart and Glenn Ford spoke of their World War II experiences, and that made the evening even more somber.

When Jimmy Stewart and Glenn Ford were finished individually thanking the guests, who by this time were getting a little sleepy, the music started playing Mae's theme song, "A Pretty Girl Is Like a Melody." Now Ms. West was not a young woman at that time, and it took a couple of times through the song till she finally made her way up front. The audience applauded as she climbed up on the stage. She raised the obelisk in her hand and said, "This is the hardest thing I've held in my hands in a long time!" She left the stage to an ovation I haven't heard since.

Another time, I remember doing a home party in the San Fernando Valley. As I normally do, I stayed close to the front door as guests arrived so I could alert the bartenders when I knew one of the guests liked a certain drink so we would have it ready for them. For example, Elizabeth Taylor liked Jack Daniels or Champagne.

Among the guests at this event was Tim Conway from *McHale's Navy* and *The Carol Burnett Show.* We had known each other over the years, and Tim would always come over to me to compliment me on the food or decor or just to say hello.

This day as Tim entered, he saw me and told me that when he saw my truck and gave his car to the valet parking attendant, he knew it was going to be a fun affair—except we did not have valet parking. Tim had given his brand-new car to a complete stranger, who must have been somewhat surprised to say the least.

I believe everything worked out fine.

Then there was the time when Universal Studios in California had just opened a corporate tented facility, and Carousel was the first catering service to use it. I was looking for a facility that was new and different for a new client that was a meeting planner for an organization that raised money for children. She was the latest to volunteer for that job, and because we had worked for her in the past, she asked me to look for a unique place for this event. She also said in the past it had always been in a hotel that had a room for cocktails and a separate room for dinner. After speaking to my Universal contact, they were anxious to get this event and claimed they would have all celebrities who were scheduled on the night of the event make an appearance.

The meeting planner was really excited and sold the idea to her board, and they accepted. Well, at least the board did!

With contracts signed and the deposit in the bank, I decided I wanted to go to Paris and buy a new tuxedo from Ted Lepidus so I would look fabulous the night of the event, while also taking a long-needed vacation.

I realized after I arrived in France that as soon as I spoke a word, the price would be go up. I pretended that I was a deaf mute and got my $600 tuxedo for $150 and a small glass of sherry. My mother would have been proud.

On the night of the event, it was a little breezy, but the tent overlooked downtown LA on one side and the San Fernando Valley on the other—a really gorgeous view.

As I said, the board approved of the tent at Universal, but most of the guests did not. There was no ballroom, no separate room for cocktails, and they complained about how chilly it was. But we were already set with tables, chairs, and even the first course, which was a beautiful romaine wedge with homemade green goddess dressing.

I was in the kitchen area, supervising dish-up for the main course of filet of beef, when a waiter rushed in and told me that there was a guest who was making a scene. I thought I would go out and see what was wrong and calm things down. This woman—I was going to call her a lady, but she sure wasn't—did not like the tent or anything else for that matter.

When I arrived at her table in my Ted Lepidus tuxedo, I asked politely if I could be of service. She answered, "I won't speak to a *nobody*. I want to know why we are at this table when I am always up front!"

A little mad about being called a "nobody," I retorted, "I would think that one would buy a table at functions like this to help kids, not complain about where they are sitting."

She freaked out and slammed her husband's green goddess salad in my face, and it ran down onto my new tuxedo.

I told her what I thought of her, and she hit me with *her* salad this time.

I was so mad, and other guests, including the meeting planner, were furious! It was spiraling out of control. So I went to the stage, grabbed the microphone, and ordered all Carousel to leave the floor and we never served one meal. The party was over.

We later got sued by the client. But the meeting planner, testifying at the hearing that the client had asked for new ideas and that Carousel had done its best, won the case for us.

PS: my tuxedo was ruined.

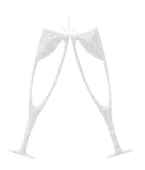

"Trouble in Paradise"

Paradise to my partner, Steven, and me, of course, was Palm Springs. In the late 1970s, after visiting there, we decided to invest in a condo and become weekend desert warriors. We already owned a house in Van Nuys, California, business was good, and we were traveling all through the country doing events. So we purchased this little home away from home to relax whenever we could get out there.

Around 1984, after taking a shower, I noticed a small lump under my left arm. I thought little about it until it grew larger (the size of a small lemon), so I decided to see my doctor back home in the San Fernando Valley. He made the appointment with a specialist, and after a diagnosis, it was determined that I had lymphoma cancer. They did a biopsy through which I was sedated. As I started to wake in the hospital room, I thought I saw my partner, Steven, sitting on the edge of the bed while wearing all black. Subconsciously, I was obviously very worried.

Soon the doctor walked in and said, "You have cancer, and it doesn't look good."

I was having a hard time taking in everything the doctor was saying while I was keeping an eye on Steven, who looked like he was going to faint. I heard the doctor continue that there was no guarantee but we should try chemo and radiation and, if needed, spinal taps. I replied, "Why don't you stop talking and start the treatments?"

He was not a pleasant man, and at that point, I was out of patience as well. I was used to watching Dr. Welby-type doctors on TV, and he was more like Judge Judy, but I went along because I wanted to beat this, and I wanted to do it now. It turned out that it was his way of helping to cure patients, namely making them so mad at him that they fought the cancer almost as a way to get even. I've got to tell you I was more than mad at him, but it worked, and here I am today all these years later with no cancer.

During the treatments, which lasted about eight months, my primary doctor had a long talk with Steven and me and suggested that if there was someplace we always wanted to go, we should do it. He further told me to turn in any savings and IRAs and make the company solvent for Steven. I followed his advice, but then I lived. I was thinking of suing for malpractice. Just kidding.

Since Carousel had already started to cater in Palm Springs, it was easy to work from home in our new condo. So in between going to LA for treatments, I sought out more catering in Palm Springs and got quite a few jobs. A neighbor told me that he had some marijuana and gave me a joint to smoke if my stomach got upset from the chemo.

Carousel had a job for a huge oil company that had rented six celebrity homes for dinner on the same evening, and of course, I was in charge of one dinner. That morning, I felt like I was going to heave all over the condo, and suddenly I remembered the joint in my bedside table so I smoked it—all of it.

It worked as my nausea left and I was feeling no pain at all, but I couldn't even walk. I had to ask for a lift to the party. The owner of the home was a locally known radio host, and when he saw me, he knew immediately that I was stoned out of my mind and put me in a director's chair so I could yell instructions to my crew. Thank God by the time the guests arrived I was a little better, but I stayed in the chair.

Carousel became the preferred caterer in Palm Springs for venues, such as the Empire Polo Club, the Palm Springs Air Museum, and many more, and some of those venues still call us today for events. So I believe the thought *Gratitude changes attitude* has kept me well after two more bouts with cancer—prostate and kidney, and open-heart surgery.

Every Day Should
Be Thanksgiving

Several years after having our own office and kitchen, and while doing very well and beginning to realize Carousel was well-known and respected, I noticed that the month of November was never a lucrative month, maybe because it was before the holidays or the weather was turning chilly.

In fact, the only holiday in November was Thanksgiving, so one day I thought, *Maybe families are not the market to reach out to. After all, I am gay and also I can't cook, so there had to be thousands like me in the San Fernando Valley and Hollywood.* The team and I got together and designed a very nice box that would contain a twenty-pound, fully cooked turkey with chestnut stuffing, candied yams, homemade giblet gravy, and pumpkin pie. It was sized to serve twelve guests, and the cost was sixty dollars including delivery the morning of Thanksgiving.

We placed small ads in the *Hollywood Reporter* and *Variety*. Those were both show business magazines, and the gay crowd we were after was either in the business or wanted to be.

In case it was a bad idea, and to protect Carousel's name, I called it The American Princess with a tag that said simply "I'm tired already." A month before Thanksgiving, we had just seven orders, and I figured this was not working out to be a good idea. However, three weeks before the big day, we were up to 750 orders, and it was turning out to be *too* good an idea. Fear struck. *Where are we going to cook all those turkeys, and how are we going to deliver them?*

Steven started to go around to neighborhood bakeries, Jewish temples, friends' homes, and restaurants to enlist help. We had to hire several chefs from a local labor provider, but it worked out and we delivered 750 very nicely packaged turkey dinners on Thanksgiving Day, according to plan.

On Thanksgiving Day and after delivering a portion of those dinners, Steven had to go to his parents and asked me to start our dinner for twelve friends. He said to just follow the instructions that were inside the box. When our boxed Carousel dinner arrived, Steven was stuck in traffic so I started the dinner alone. All was fine until I started to carve the turkey and noticed something strange. It turned out that the chef had not taken out the bag of giblets from inside the turkey. Gross! I thought, *If I got the bag, who else got the bag?* And I soon found out.

We went to the office the next day and called everyone on the list. Fortunately very few got the bag, but Peggy Lee was pissed and sued us. Milton Berle got the bag but told me he did twenty minutes entertaining his guests about it. Joan Rivers was very pleasant about it and commented that all was fine.

Today, turkey dinners like ours are sold in grocery markets across the country.

We Got Our Act Together and Took It on the Road

Our first corporate client to ask us to cater out of Los Angeles was Dr. Pepper. They were having their annual bottler's convention in LA and contacted a destination management company to arrange a catered dinner in a special place for 2,200 guests. The DMC guy contacted me and asked me if I knew of an interesting but special place that could handle that many people. So I searched and came across the Los Angeles Arboretum. It was used to film *Fantasy Island.*

The entertainment that night was Tony Bennett, and as great as he was, Carousel was also appreciated, so much so that we catered the next bottler's conventions in Las Vegas, followed by Maui, San Antonio, Palm Springs, and Chicago.

We also traveled across the country with *PC Magazine,* Hitachi, Cadillac, Sprint, and many more. I remember in the beginning, I would go to visit corporate accounts to see if we could improve our service to them in any way. All responded favorably and liked what we delivered, and the meeting planner for Hitachi answered my question by commenting, "Why don't you come to Chicago for the Consumer Electronics Show?"

Hitachi was expecting around one thousand guests at $50 a guest, a total of $50,000. So I figured, *Why not?*

I thought this first job for Hitachi in Chicago during the Consumer Electronics Show (CES) might be a little different from working in Los Angeles, and this worried me a little. But I was sure that all those trying this with me would do whatever needed to be done so the party would be a success. Well, it was for Hitachi, but not for Carousel, as we lost around $15,000.

While there, however, we saw how many events took place in Chicago and the large guest counts at these events. It was clear that we had to seek out other locations and lock them in quickly so we would be able to offer to clients our suggested menus and theme for the location of their choice. For example, for a smaller event of maybe one hundred to two hundred, the Wrigley Mansion ten minutes from downtown Chicago or the Water Tower on Michigan Avenue were memorable and exciting venues.

There was also Park Plaza, a disco close by which held over one thousand guests, and Faces Disco on Rush Street was also a favorite for many clients because it was close to all the hotels for taxis or for a short walk. And last but certainly not least was the South Shore Country Club. Meeting planners provided bus transportation back and forth at this location. And of course, one of the most prestigious locations will always be the Field Museum of Natural History.

Within a short period of time, we had a nice array of locations of all types and sizes. Now it was time to study the CES book from front to back and call each and every meeting planner listed to offer our services.

At first we got cold responses, due to the fact that Carousel was in Los Angeles while their company might have been in New Jersey, and I wanted to cater their party in Chicago. So you can understand their concerns. But I would just ask if I could send sample menus and a brochure, which we did, and out of that, we probably got seven out of ten jobs the following year.

The same procedure was repeated when CES was in Atlanta and Las Vegas.

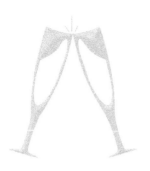

Motown

Carousel Catering has catered many events at the home of Berry Gordy, the founder of Motown Records. His home was a beautiful mansion in Beverly Hills, spacious inside as well as outside with beautiful exotic animals, such as llamas, flamingos and much, *much* more. I had the opportunity to meet all the Motown stars either at one of Berry's events or at an event for them personally.

I think in those days we catered all the events for Motown. I remember getting a call from Bob Jones, who as I remember was the head of publicity for Motown, asking me to go to the home of the Jackson 5 and arrange for a press conference in their garden. I met all the family. The Jackson family was always nice to me and my crew, and as the years went by, I saw Michael at different events that Carousel was catering. He always was cordial. He was generous, he was patient, and he was very kind.

I guess Michael was about ten years old, and he was a joy to be around. We probably catered five or six different events at that estate. We also catered the premiere of *Mahogany*, starring Diana Ross, at Berry Gordy's estate. Diana looked sensational, as did all the guests, and the garden and pool area was regally adorned in lavish decor.

Catering for a King

I received another call from Bob Jones years later telling me to go and speak to a client who, as it turned out, was a king from a nation in Africa. He lived in a beautiful mansion in Beverly Hills.

It seemed as though the king's daughter had a crush on Michael Jackson and wanted to have a dinner party at her home and invite the entire Jackson family. Now during those years, Michael and his mother were practicing Jehovah's Witnesses, and I was told by Bob that Michael would not be anywhere where there was liquor or smoking. As I was driving to the appointment, I kept thinking, *Life is a beautiful thing, and here I am going to interview a king.*

A young, self-educated man from Brooklyn about to cater a party for a king, and I'd never learned how to cook.

I was met by this very nice black man who introduced himself as the king's interpreter. We walked to a beautiful garden, and within a few minutes, a rather large man entered wearing a bejeweled kimono. I had never seen such a garment. His Majesty looked toward the pool and spoke to the interpreter, who in turn asked me if I could cover the pool for dinner service. "Of course" was my response. The king spoke again, and I was told he wanted a roof overhead too, to cover all guests. Again, I said, "Of course."

It was for about sixty guests, which included all rentals, food, service, and labor. I was sure that the Jackson family would not attend. When I was asked for an approximate cost, I thought, *If I say $150 per person all-inclusive, that would be $9,000,* but he was a king, so I asked for $250 per person. The chatter between the king and his interpreter got a little intense so I started to reach down for my attaché case, as I thought that I was going to be shown the exit. But I was informed that the price was not enough, so I said, "Okay, pick a number," and I was given $20,000 in cash—over $300 per person!

The event was a smash hit but had an interesting denouement. Shortly thereafter, there was an uproar in the king's home country, and he had to fly back to fight a civil war. Their maid, seeing an opportunity, set up her boyfriend with the queen's daughter, who ended up moving across the street into a mansion of her own. And the maid's boyfriend ended up with a new Mercedes-Benz and other prizes that one assumes the maid enjoyed as well.

PS: Michael did not show up.

Dinah Shore Golf

We catered the first nine years of the Dinah Shore LGPA golf tournament at Mission Hill Country Club in Rancho Mirage, California, providing food and beverages to all the food stations around the course. But I knew nothing about golf or the first tee from the tenth hole, so I colored-coordinated them. The LPGA officials were not too pleased, and after a while, I received a call from one of them to let me know something was needed on the yellow tent, and that was easy for me.

And then there was the golf cart incident. We were all assigned golf carts to shuttle food and beverages to the different stations. Feeling quite sure of my ability to drive a golf cart, I got caught not looking where I was going and clipped the sponsor of the event and his wife. The worst part was that I lost all the product I was carrying.

I still don't know anything about golf, but I'm good at colors. And to this day, I stay away from golf carts.

Elizabeth Taylor

I met Elizabeth Taylor in November 1968 shortly after her father died. As I said earlier, Carousel Catering was up and running, and we were respected in our community by members of the talent agencies, charities, and of course television and motion picture studios. Among these was United Artist Pictures, where we catered wrap parties as well as motion picture premieres held at the studio or the Directors Guild of America in Hollywood.

The woman who scheduled all the events for UA, Ms. Valerie Douglas, was a delight to work with and gave me much trust in delivering exactly what she wanted. We spent many times together sharing dinner in one of the local hot spots and got to know each other quite well.

One day she asked about my family and was delighted to hear that my father's family was from Cardiff, Wales. Valerie was a good friend of Richard Burton, who was then married to Elizabeth. She thought it would be a good idea to arrange a meeting the next time Richard was in town. That idea was talked about for probably two years until November 20, 1968, when Valerie called me and told me that Elizabeth's father had died and she wanted me and a small group of my staff to go up to the home of Mr. and Mrs. Taylor and stay with Sara (Elizabeth's mother) until Richard and Elizabeth returned from their chalet in Switzerland.

Valerie arrived first, followed by the Burtons, who were very pleasant as they expressed gratitude for our being there and looking after Sara. Valerie and I became fast friends. Over the years, if the Burtons were in town for any special occasion, Valerie would advise me if they required anything from Carousel. They did not have a home in California at the time, as they traveled a lot, and when they were there, they stayed in a bungalow at the Beverly Hills Hotel.

One day, Valerie called me and told me that Elizabeth was finishing up a movie and there was a wrap party planned at the studio for approximately two hundred guests. Elizabeth wanted Carousel to cater the party, so we did. Later I was told that Richard was going to present Elizabeth with the famous diamond ring when they arrived back at the bungalow during a small gathering of about fifteen guests on the same night as the wrap party, and it was to be a surprise.

However, no one told me about the surprise part, and while we were catering the wrap party, Elizabeth was at the buffet table. I whispered in her ear that we were planning a nice menu for the bungalow later and added, "So please don't eat too much." She looked at me, smiled, and said, "That was supposed to be a surprise," and continued along the buffet line.

OMG.

I thought, What if she says something to Richard? Valerie and all involved would probably fire me or just never use our services again. I had a staff at the bungalow and of course staff at the studio wrap party, so I left early and headed to the bungalow. I hoped that it would not be as bad as I thought it might be.

Valerie was informed when Elizabeth's car was leaving the studio and when the car was getting close to the bungalow, so the surprise would work. The car finally arrived, the door opened, and when Elizabeth entered, the invited guests gave her a large round of applause. She acted surprised, graciously thanked everybody, looked at me, and smiled.

Phew.

Passion for Women Perfume

After a few years, I was introduced to Chen Sam, Elizabeth's publicist. Chen was known as Elizabeth's mouthpiece. She was a beautiful lady from South Africa and was adored by Elizabeth. The feeling, of course, was mutual.

We ended up catering all the launch parties for Elizabeth's new perfume lines, Passion for Women and Passion for Men. I was very pleased and proud to have been given the opportunity to coordinate all those events in so many major cities across the country. She was wonderful to all who traveled with her and it was magical to witness how adored she was by so many.

My responsibilities were not only providing food but also getting the best locations available in each city where the perfume was launched, as well as coordinating music, florals, and so on. When the cities were chosen—mostly through Carousel's database of locations around the country—Chen and I would get on a plane and visit several sites. She would choose one that met her needs, such as egress and ingress and a place for members of the press, and I would figure out how we'd set up and what we needed in the way of food and service.

The first launch for Passion for Women was held in Beverly Hills. Chen asked me to find a place close to where Elizabeth lived, as she was historically late in arriving at events. Fortunately, I had the answer. The former home of Kenny Rogers, now belonging to Mark Hughes, the owner of Herbalife, was only three houses away from Elizabeth's. Mark agreed to take on the event, even though he was going to be in Maui.

The press had an area outside the front door, and when her limo arrived, the cameras lit up the whole courtyard as some four hundred guests awaited her arrival. Hors d'oeuvres and cocktails were followed by an Italian dinner, which was Elizabeth's favorite.

She was only a little late.

The second Passion for Women event took place at Sotheby's in New York, a beautiful location that Macy's decorated completely in purple (Elizabeth's favorite color), including linens, chairs, and a long purple carpet leading inside the auction house. Elizabeth arrived on a purple motorcycle, wearing a purple motorcycle jacket. Her driver, also wearing the same jacket, was her friend, Malcolm Forbes.

The first launch party for Passion for Men was held at the New York Stock Exchange, and the second was during an NFL football game in Dallas Stadium, Texas. Our Carousel traveling team had use of Jerry Jones's private box, from where we watched Elizabeth toss the coin and begin the game. As she walked onto the field and was announced, the applause and roar from the crowd literally shook the box.

It was a terrific experience, and at a time when I had only one more thing to ask of her.

Elizabeth Taylor with Bill Jones

Elizabeth Taylor and the AIDS Epidemic

Carousel Catering was still moving along doing corporate events across the country, and one day a friend of mine, Jack Hamilton, called me and asked if I would do him a small favor. Jack was a fairly well-known psychologist and was dealing primarily with the gay society, offering counseling to young people who had trouble dealing with a number of issues that go along with being gay.

Jack told me that because friends of his were dying from a no-name disease, other friends of his had started a foundation called AIDS Project Los Angeles (APLA), and they were planning a fundraiser gala and would like me to go over to the project and help with menu planning and whatever else I could offer. It was during the late eighties and people were dying in numbers, but no one knew why, so these guys, and soon the entire gay community, pitched in wherever needed.

I called APLA and set up an appointment to see them a few days later. After a short discussion, they told me the gala was to be in about six or seven months at the Century

Plaza Hotel. I said I would be happy to work with the hotel chef to be sure they were getting a good deal, but then the shoe dropped. They wanted me to ask Elizabeth Taylor to present or accept an award.

Chen Sam had told me that Elizabeth did not like accepting recognition for anything if it was not deserved. That sort of thing really bothered her. And to this point, Elizabeth had not been involved in the AIDS issue. I explained to the APLA guys that I would try but there would be no guarantees.

I thought long and hard about whether I was going to approach Elizabeth, and if so, what would I say. I called Chen in New York, told her the whole story, and she suggested we set up a meeting with Elizabeth at the house. We did so, and after telling her about what this foundation was trying to accomplish, and maybe because she knew Rock Hudson was dealing with it as well, she agreed to help. She stated that she would not accept an award but would present it to Betty Ford instead.

I was thrilled that I had gone to see Elizabeth to help APLA, and now we had not only one powerful woman but two. When we went to press, tickets were sold out almost immediately; in fact, the gala had to be moved to a different hotel because the ticket sales doubled. Elizabeth Taylor gave a face to AIDS and eventually raised tons of money for AIDS research.

She took over the event completely and ran the whole shebang, including Chen's staff, my staff, and other volunteers. All worked night and day to see that APLA's first Commitment to Life gala was a success, and it was.

The rest, as they say, is history. In a book called The Most Beautiful Woman in the World, Elizabeth talks about this and how she got involved with AIDS.

Elizabeth Taylor, Betty Ford, and Steven Ramirez

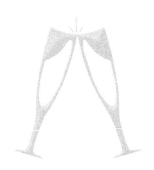

The Puppy

Elizabeth was a dedicated animal lover. She had a cat named Chole and a little dog so small you could have put it in a small bag. The cat belonged to Chen originally, but she traveled so much for and with Elizabeth she thought it would not be fair leaving Chole alone, even though some of Chen's staff looked after Chole when Chen was not home in New York.

After Chen spoke to Elizabeth about it, Elizabeth decided that Chole should stay at her house and Elizabeth's staff would look after her and she would never be alone. The cat lived a long time and had a good life, to say the least.

Bob Hope used to host the Humanitarian of the Year awards at the McCallum Theatre in Rancho Mirage, California. I believe it was the mid-eighties when the prestigious award was presented to Elizabeth Taylor.

There were many famous people who attended this event, which included celebrities, politicians, and other notables. Among the celebrities who stood on stage to celebrate the life of Elizabeth Taylor was actor Charles Bronson. After telling all of us in the audience how giving and loving Elizabeth was to so many people over the years, he finished his talk by handing her a beautiful puppy. Elizabeth was thrilled to tears and never let go of that puppy for the rest of the evening. Due to the fact that everyone was about to go on the road, the puppy was sent by limo to Elizabeth's Bel Air home, where she cared for and loved him along with the rest of her animals.

More Support for AIDS

C arousel had donated food to raise money for AIDS organizations like Aid for AIDS and Shanti, but these events were on a small level in someone's garden or a gay bar somewhere. When we felt it would help the cause to have a famous person attend, I called on my friend John Bowab, who at that time was producing shows like *The Facts of Life, The Cosby Show,* and many more. Never saying no, he would call a show business friend, and someone would always show up for us.

In 2000, John bought a huge home in the Hollywood Hills and suggested to me that we could host thirty or forty guests in his living room each month and raise money for the AIDS cause. John donated the house and sometimes the valet parking, and Carousel donated the food left over from other catered events and the labor.

Tickets were sold at one hundred dollars for dinner and a show that included all of the above. It wasn't long before guests were calling to see what celebrity would be appearing next. We had names such as Barbara Cook, Nancy Dussault, Betty Buckley, Jim Baily, Maureen Reagan, Patricia Morison, and so many more. Needless to say, the 30 to 40 guest count became 150 to 200, and we held it for about three years.

Steven

It was October 17, 1975, at about 3:15 in the afternoon, at a home in Beverly Hills when I first laid eyes on who I knew was the most beautiful man I had ever seen. He had stunning, shiny black hair down his back, bronze skin, and brown eyes. I had promised myself that until I was a complete success I would not come out to the public, but I became so nervous and excited that I had to go into the kitchen and just watch him from afar. He came with the florist and along with his boss did all necessary floral decor and tent decorations. When they finished and left, I was a little relieved, as I could not pay attention to anything else. So when we were through with our setup, I changed into my tuxedo and prepared to run the event.

Guests started to arrive soon after, and to my surprise, so did Steven, now wearing a beautiful black suit, along with his boss. He looked incredible. I, of course, went back to the kitchen and watched the entire event from a bay window. I noticed that his boss was very outgoing and knew most of the guests, but Steven stayed by himself, had one or two drinks, and danced with the hostess's daughter.

I began setting up the dessert table, which was in their game room on a covered pool table. I turned at a noise, and there he was, kind of tipsy. He said, "I have been looking for you." But before I could answer, he forced me on top of the English trifle and the chocolate mousse and kissed me for what seemed like forever. I was loving it but also worried about the desserts and my tuxedo.

That was day one of a twenty-two-year love affair. There were good years and bad years but always love years. I remember the hostess, who knew me from other events we had catered, apologizing and offering to pay for the cleaning of my tuxedo. At the end of the evening, she approached me and asked if I could have one of the valet attendants drive Steven home, as he was sitting on her front lawn. I replied I would take care of it!

Steven was seventeen years younger than me and suffered a lot of joking when someone asked him where and how we met. He would answer, "At a bar mitzvah," and of course the reply was always "Was it yours?" I would have people tell me how lucky Steven was in meeting a successful man with an established business. My answer was always that when Steven joined Chef David in the kitchen, they took Carousel Catering from being a good company to a great company because of their love for trying new dishes found in food and wine magazines.

Easter Sunday of 1998, Steven made his transition at the age of forty-one due to complications from AIDS.

It was a very nervous time to be gay and deal with the misunderstanding of this no-name disease. People didn't know if they could be infected by shaking someone's hand, touching their silverware, or by just coughing. Nobody knew except that it was a gay disease. A friend of ours had a very successful catering company in West Hollywood and catered some very fancy house parties. But the panic was so great, and because (I suspect) all her help were very handsome gay men, clients stopped calling and she went out of business.

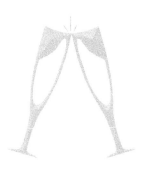

How We Met Chef David

Steven and I had been together for almost four years when one day he told me that a new country-western bar called the Raw Hide was offering line dancing with live country-western bands every weekend. So after dinner one Saturday, we decided to stop by and see what it was all about.

It was a nice, friendly bar, clean, with nice patrons, and the music was very good. The bartender was a tall, heavyset man, very friendly, and was called Big Myrna. He was in command of his territory as well as the rest of the bar staff. On Sundays, they always had a beer bust, and Myrna would place a pot of chili on the bar. It was the best chili I had ever tasted.

On the way home, Steven and I both expressed a desire to see if Myrna (David) would like to join our team at Carousel. But it wasn't until after being invited to dinner at David's home that we decided to ask him, as he showed great creativity in the meal he served. For example, the first course was a soup served in a miniature ceramic toilet bowl; the entree was a beef stew served in a ceramic bathtub, and the dessert was served in a martini glass. Of course, the cloth napkins were bar towels.

We knew then that he would be a good fit, so we asked, and he came on board, at first as a bartender working events and then joining Steven and the rest of the staff in the kitchen. When I think back, David never knew anything about catering, yet he took command of the kitchen and today cooks for thousands.

From that first night in the bar, Steven had taken a liking to Myrna, and as it turned out, we not only worked many years together but we all became fast friends.

Lesson learned: never judge people, because you never know what they can contribute one day.

Chef David's Memories

(In David's Own Words)

Story 1

There are too many memories to put in one chapter or even one book, but one thing that I will always remember is how we've grown and how today we think things out carefully before we do any event.

For example, one of the first jobs I worked on with Bill was for Dr. Pepper held at the Los Angeles Arboretum in the *Fantasy Island* area. Because I had experience as a bartender, Bill put me in charge of setting up fifteen bars complete with all the alcohol as well as ice and every imaginable Dr. Pepper product, and there were many.

Bartenders were hired for the evening, and the fifteen bars were set up in time and ready when all guests arrived, except that Bill forgot to mention one small detail. After the cocktail hour, all these bars had to be moved from the cocktail area to the dining area. I wanted to choke him, but we all got together and saw that some bars were moved over and were available to the guests at dinnertime. Soon after that, we decided to place satellite bars and wine stations in areas where necessary.

Then there was the four-day journey for the Seagram's Corporation. A meeting planner based in New Orleans for whom we had worked in the past called and asked if we could provide food, labor, and all party equipment needed for the Seagram's events.

The schedule was to be as follows:

- Day 1: Arrival in Los Angeles of all food, drinks, and labor handled by the hotel.

- Day 2: All guests were to board a special bus that would transport them to the first stop—a seven-hour bus ride to Saratoga, California. Snacks, drinks, and light food were to be served on the bus. We arranged to have a beautiful lunch in the gardens of the Montalvo Arts Center as well as a twenty-piece orchestra playing opera and show tunes. My staff was always ahead of the bus so we could set up and dress buffet tables and prepare all foods.

As I stated, we were ahead of the bus. In fact, we were there the night before, and thank God we were. Informed that Montalvo had a kitchen, we found out when we got there that it didn't. Panic struck until we remembered that our motel suite was complete with a small kitchenette and dishwasher. So with little time to waste, we went back to the hotel and started cooking potatoes, pasta, and green beans, all which would be made into salads the next morning.

Because the stove had only two burners, we decided to poach the salmon in the dishwasher. Don't ask me how I knew this would work, but thank God it did. By the end of the day, we were exhausted between hustling back and forth to our van, where everything was iced down in an ice chest, and cooking all that food for about seventy guests.

Arriving at Montalvo the next day under beautiful sunshine, we were told that the buffets would be set up in the middle of a flowering garden. The gardens were incredible, and the colors of the tablecloths shone brightly in the sun. As guests arrived, so did a swarm of bees that were heading for the buffets. We set up fans, and those as well as the staff's flailing arms kept the bees at bay, for the most part.

We couldn't stay to hear the orchestra, but I was told later all guests loved the facility as well as the food and music.

Lesson learned: bees like salmon.

Story 2

On another occasion, we were to cater an event at Beach Blanket Babylon in San Francisco, the world's longest running musical revue and one of the most popular San Francisco attractions with its high-energy, pop culture satire.

We were about three hours ahead of the guests who would experience the show and dinner.

Upon arrival and starting the setup along with my staff, we realized that we had left behind six sauté pans we needed for sautéing medallions of beef—and for chicken masala at lunch. No problem. We knew we had some time as the guests, when arriving in San Francisco, would be taken to their hotel and rest before coming to Beach Blanket for the show and dinner.

There were plenty of restaurants along the wharf, so we started to go from one to another to beg chefs to let us use six sauté pans for the day. After a few turndowns, we finally found a chef who was gracious enough to see our problem and let us borrow six sauté pans. Today he is a close friend.

The client wanted fresh seafood from the San Francisco Fish Market, and the theater was on the wharf, so we figured we were in good shape. However, our experience was less than favorable as the salespeople were reluctant to sell us the amount of seafood we needed. I asked the purveyor, "Do you have 150 oysters?"

He replied, "Yes."

I said, "I'll take them."

He said, "But then I won't have any more for my customers!"

I said, "I am one of your customers. I'll take 150 oysters, 450 jumbo shrimp, and fifty pounds of halibut, and you will be done for the day!"

He saw the logic in that, and we were in business.

The staff at Babylon was terrific to work with, the show was incredible, and the guests were thrilled.

Story 3

We had to decide how we were going to travel from city to city so it would make sense. The decision was that we would plan on being in any city well in advance of the event to catch any potential problems in advance, such as delays in airlines, forgetting an important piece of equipment, or something requested by the client that must be there. How far in advance we arrived (five days, a week, whatever) depended on the size of each event and the location.

For example, for Dr. Pepper on Maui, it was two weeks before to prep and one week after for rest and recuperation; for the Summer Olympics in Atlanta, it was almost one month of prep. All costs were built into the budget long before any event was finalized.

Then there were the two simultaneous events in New Orleans, one a seated dinner for 180 guests at the beautiful Long View Gardens just outside the French Quarter, complete with mini Mardi Gras parade. And the other was for one hundred guests seated for a dinner at the Float Warehouse, where all the floats for Mardi Gras were made.

The Float Warehouse event was late in the afternoon, and when that was over, most of the Carousel staff had to get on a plane for an event for Toshiba that was held at the Museum of High Art on the following evening in Atlanta. I was left with a smaller core crew, so we added more temporary staff to fill the gap. However, the temporary staff left a lot to be desired in professionalism and Carousel had to finish the job on our own, cooking, serving, cleaning up, and getting the unused liquor back to where it was purchased. While the staff was checking the liquor, local staff who had already left would run back, grab a bottle of booze, and run into the woods. This must have happened fifteen times: run, grab a bottle, and run back into the woods.

By the time I was through cleaning up, and after dropping my remaining staff back at the hotel, returning the rented truck, and shipping all equipment back to Los Angeles, it was about 4:00 a.m. I had to be up by 7:00 a.m. to catch a plane to Atlanta, which arrived at 9:00 a.m., for the Toshiba party that started eight hours later. We were logistics experts, but maybe a little sleep deprived.

Lesson learned: just because one wears a uniform or an apron doesn't mean one is a soldier or a server.

Herbalife

One of the special events people at Universal Studios was Kathy, a young woman full of fun and kind of wild. We had gotten a lot of business at the Studios due to her. But after several years, Kathy had left her job.

Four or five years later, my phone rang, and it was Kathy. She explained that she had been working in Tokyo for a clothing designer but was now working for a firm in LA that sold health food. She explained that her boss was planning a party for five hundred guests and wanted a fruit display, and she felt we did the best in town.

I was beginning to question why anybody would want just a fruit display and thought she was a little dingy after such a long time in Tokyo, so I figured I'd give her a ridiculously high price and that would be that. I priced the fruit display at $15,000. She didn't blink an eye and said she would talk to her boss and get back to me. Her boss was Mark Hughes, the founder of Herbalife.

It turned out that after accepting the fruit display, he wanted more like ribs, chicken, and an "incredible" BBQ (his words). Now I was in a panic mode because if I charged him $15,000 for a fruit display, what must I charge for a complete high-end BBQ? Anyway, he seemed unfazed by cost. I know he spent over $60,000 for the event and loved it.

That was the begging of our association with Mark and Herbalife, and it lasted for about five years catering Herbalife conventions in Atlanta at the Fox Theater and many at his home in Bel Air on his tennis court. We also catered his wedding on Maui, another wedding celebration at the home, and a cocktail reception at the Riviera Country Club in Bel Air. The bride was a former Ms. Sweden and was a very beautiful woman. Mark was a very handsome man who dressed himself in only tailor-made suits.

Always at the Herbalife conventions, he would enter with the band playing *Rocky* music, his fist high over his head, a huge smile, and the crowd standing and applauding. It was quite a spectacle. After that entry, we served the famous Herbalife juice bar using all company products and whatever they decided to serve for their guests.

I remember having dinner with Mark's second in command in Hawaii and hearing her state that they would not have a million-dollar quarter. Ohhh!

Lessons Learned by Accident

I took pride in trying different things to create new business. Because I didn't know how to cook or the difference between a Cuisinart and a can opener, I always felt a little weird being the owner of a catering company. But I always remembered things of importance told to me by others who were far more intelligent.

One man in particular, whom I mentioned earlier in the book, was Bob Lieberman, my first boss in Los Angeles. He would tell me, "Never say no. If a client asked if you have any experience in certain matters, just always say yes, and then find a way to get it done."

A good example is the couscous story. The client asked if we make a good couscous, and of course I said yes, not having a clue as to what she was talking about. She eventually gave me the recipe from a chef in Morocco, and voila! I not only knew what it was, but we could make a darn good one.

Unfortunately sometimes radical things happen before you find a way to accomplish what you were trying to do. For example, we were catering a party for Elizabeth Taylor in a home they rented after the filming of *Night of the Iguana*. It was supposed to be held in the large garden, but it was pouring down rain.

Elizabeth came down and wanted a glass of Jack Daniels. As the bartender was pouring it, I noticed a puddle of rainwater in the corner of the roof of the tent. So showing off in front Elizabeth, I did what I witnessed many rental guys do in cases like this. I picked up a broomstick and pressed it to the tent top to push the water down the side. Unfortunately, it did not go down the side of the tent, but all over Ms. Taylor and the bartender.

Disaster!

But then again, how many people can say they dumped a bucket of rainwater on Elizabeth Taylor?

And being the loving person she was, she forgave me.

A Hole in the Ground

I t became clear to Steven and me in the early stages of Carousel that a big hole in the ground (excavation) meant something will eventually be built. So when we had the time, we would drive around Los Angeles, San Diego, and sometimes even Santa Barbara, looking for holes in the ground. As time went by, a construction team would show up and start construction. Then we would ask what was going up and call that company immediately to ask to submit a bid for catering services. We often got hired, sometimes for a ribbon cutting ceremony and sometimes for a huge grand opening.

I remember driving around Hollywood with Steven when he noticed on the corner of Sunset and Vine there was a big hole in the ground. We kept watch, and it soon became apparent that it was going to be a new Home Savings & Loan. We contacted their PR department and after a short time were asked to bid. The PR department had some very specific requirements, such as because it was located in Hollywood on such a prestigious corner, they wanted a Hollywood theme. I thought, *What can you do with a Hollywood theme inside a bank?*

The fun now was starting.

We decided to do research on the property and maybe get some ideas for a theme, and in studying the land the bank was standing on, we discovered that it was once a motion picture studio. And if I remember correctly, it was used for *How the West Was Won* interior shots. So we found our theme and won the bid.

I can't remember how many guests attended the event, but I know there were hundreds. Outside the building, we coordinated a fashion show where the Edith Head Studio costume designer featured models wearing clothes she made for different movies over the years. We also had men and women lookalikes, such as Clark Gable, Marilyn Monroe, Bette Davis, Charlie Chapman, and more.

It was very successful, and we went on to cater many openings for Home Savings & Loan.

Another time, while driving around Century City, we discovered a huge hole that turned out to be the Twin Towers. We did the usual, found out who to call, and offered our services. We got no response until one day we received a call from a representative of a large law firm saying they got our information from building management. They were taking over two floors of the building and wanted to hold a Christmas party for clients and employees on one of the unfinished floors.

After studying the space, it was a blank canvas, and if they had the budget, there were several different ways we could go. The choice was *A Christmas Story*. Guests entered the front office by going through pages of a giant book.

Once they entered, they were met by Tiny Tim, Scrooge, and the setting of the house in which Tiny Tim lived. The food prepared was all British, and girl and boy workers were dressed as little maids and maidens, attired in fashion from that period.

One day while driving to Palm Springs, right off the I-10 Freeway was another big hole about ten blocks long. It turned out to be another shopping mall being built by the Hahn Company. They knew us from our work with them on the Fashion Valley mall in San Diego, so we had a good chance. We bid and were awarded the event, with a guest count around fifteen thousand.

All from a hole in the ground, and for years we went hole searching.

We were living proof of the value of out-of-the-box thinking—or out-of-the-hole in this case.

John Wayne

I remember Channel 4 was scheduling a special television event where it would be the first time that George Burns and Jack Benny appeared together. So I was asked to find a special location that would be of interest for this cocktail party. I suggested the *Grey Goose,* John Wayne's yacht, only because I had heard so much about it and was a big fan of Mr. Wayne.

The head of publicity for RCA was Mort Fleishman. He liked me for I had done many parties for him over the years. He called John, and they agreed on a price for the use of his yacht. All seemed fine, except when we arrived in Newport Harbor, where the *Grey Goose* was docked, I was a little disappointed at what we saw: an old mine sweeper, not a yacht.

The galley and the dining area were beautiful as well as the sleeping quarters, but the decks were kind of shabby.

When Mort asked me what I could do, I started to make suggestions, like covering the upper and lower decks with grass matting, covering the upper deck with a canopy, and placing large ficus trees as a focal point plus bringing in some chairs.

As I was making suggestions, a voice from the deck above shouted, "Get that little fluff off my boat!" But Mort had already paid the fee for the *Grey Goose* and took all my suggestions. The event was successful, and John Wayne stayed home.

Jimmy Komack

Jimmy was a major television producer, including *The Courtship of Eddie's Father, Chico and the Man*, and *Welcome Back, Kotter*, to name a few. We had catered many events for the Komacks, and while planning one event, his wife wanted to step it up a bit by having a wine tasting for their guests before dinner. Jimmy was totally against this as his favorite restaurant in West Los Angeles had a sommelier he felt was snobby and did not want his guests to be uncomfortable. I tried to explain that we had worked with some very nice sommeliers on many occasions, but Jimmy just didn't want it. So I suggested that the next time they were planning to go to that restaurant, let me know in advance as I would like to join them.

Most sommeliers, I was told by one I had worked with over the years, were first waiters, and he and I would chuckle about how people would smile while learning about the different wines offered at a tasting, get a little intoxicated, and forget the whole thing the next morning.

Anyway, I got a call from Jimmy's assistant and was told of a scheduled dinner meeting at his favorite restaurant and he wanted me there. I agreed and met them.

After we were seated for dinner, the waiter took our order and left the table. Then Jimmy's not so favorite sommelier came by and said, "Very nice to see you again, Mr. Komack. Would you like to see the wine list?" Jimmy explained that his friend Bill would be ordering the wine, so he came over to me. I immediately suggested to the sommelier that he find out from our waiter what we had ordered to eat and bring the best wine that paired with our orders. You could see him beginning to fluster, so I knew I had him.

A little time had passed when he came back with a very nice bottle of wine and showed it to me. I acknowledged that it would do. He started to pour a taste in my glass and placed the cork in front of me. I asked, "What are you doing? There's a lady at this table." He looked at me and said, "But sir, it is customary since you ordered the wine to be the first to taste the wine."

I could see he was taken off guard, so I continued to explain as I held the cork in my hand that an experienced vintner would never put an expensive cork in a mediocre bottle of wine and wine corks can be very expensive. A good cork is based on the number of lines at the bottom.

At this point, Jimmy says, "Let me see that cork." He says, "It looks like three lines, so that must be a good wine." The now totally bewildered sommelier smiled and excused himself.

Jimmy was so impressed, saying that he didn't know I knew so much about wine. I assured him I didn't. It was only a ploy and that the sommelier would probably be nicer to him the next time.

Screaming for Days

Carousel was hired to provide lunch for a group of 150 to 175 guests who were attending a Primal Therapy session. The course was to last four consecutive days, and our catering setup was in the parking lot. We were asked to be as quiet as possible during the session and not to be alarmed if we heard screams as that was part of the therapy.

Well, that was fine with me and my staff as we had been doing events for years in some of the homes in Beverly Hills where yelling and screaming were normal. So we did our job as instructed, setting the tables and chairs up very quietly and delicately and putting on the linens and glassware. Of course, there were the screams, but having been warned, we as good soldiers just carried on doing what we had been hired to do.

One day, I think it was the last day, the screaming reached a crescendo pitch and was a little nerve-racking, but we continued working. When lunchtime arrived I, as instructed, opened the door to the parking lot as the guests came down from upstairs, most with tears rolling down their faces.

One lady was still screaming as she approached me, so thinking I would comfort her, I said, "Now nothing can be that bad." She looked at me still sobbing and said, "I am half a woman!" Not sure how to react, I replied, "So am I, but it's okay."

She burst into laughter as I did. But the doctor in charge was not happy, and for some reason, we were never hired again.

Chuck Berry, Catalina Casino, and Herbalife

C arousel received another call from the meeting planner for Herbalife Nutrition telling us that they were planning a Christmas party for eight hundred Herbalife distributors and guests. But Mark Hughes, the founder, wanted a unique facility around the Los Angeles area and it was already in September, which left little time to secure any location for Christmas.

We started the process of calling and asking anyone who might know of a place that might suit our needs, but to no avail. One day while browsing through a magazine, I came across an ad for the Catalina Casino in Avalon Bay on Santa Catalina Island, twenty-six miles off the coast of southern California.

I had been to Catalina before and saw the beautiful, round building that wasn't a gambling facility, but I paid little attention to it. Herbalife, however, showed a great deal of interest when I suggested it to their meeting planner. She told me that this was a very special event and asked us to secure as entertainment Chuck Berry, the famous singer songwriter who wrote "Maybelline," "Roll over Beethoven," and "Johnny Be Good," among other rock 'n' roll hits.

We secured the Catalina Casino and Chuck Berry and started the planning when we realized that all rental equipment, such as tables, chairs, linens, china, and cutlery, had to be sent over by barges. And if the waters were rough, the barge would turn around and return to the mainland. That was a little unnerving, but we had no choice so we plowed ahead. Sometimes you just have to go for it and trust that all will work out.

I don't remember the exact amount of ferries it took to transport guests, entertainers, and personnel from the harbor in San Pedro to Catalina, but all went well. And eventually guests, entertainment, and food arrived and the party began.

The party took place on the second level of the ballroom. Mark arrived walking up the winding staircase to the second level to the theme from the *Rocky* movie. The crowd erupted in applause and screamed as always at these meetings.

The ballroom was decorated like a Christmas wonderland, and all buffets looked like huge Christmas presents using gold, silver, and red Mylar.

Chuck Berry was just what was needed as the music was terrific and the crowd danced and sang with the band until almost midnight.

The party was over and all involved were pleased; however, had it been a New Year celebration instead of Christmas that year, it would have been a different story. For less than a week later, that whole second floor collapsed down to the level below.

Lesson learned: always count your blessings.

The Consumer Electronics Show in Atlanta, Georgia

Now that we had some experience with CES in Chicago, the planning was focused on Atlanta, going through the exhibiter book, and calling companies from the first page till the last. While Steven, Robert, and I went down to Atlanta to see about locations that would work for clients as in Chicago.

We found that Atlanta is a bit smaller than Chicago, but the locations were very similar. For example, Chicago had the Field Museum for large events, Atlanta had the High Museum of Art, and there were many venues that were perfect for smaller events, like the Cyclorama in Grant Park that gave guests a cycloramic view of the burning of Atlanta during the famous Civil War battle. Longer then a football field and standing forty feet tall, it now sits in its new home at the Atlanta Civil War Museum.

Carousel was fortunate to have gotten several more new customers while in Atlanta, one being the meeting planner for Toshiba whose other clients included Adobe, Toshiba, and Microsoft. She took Carousel all over doing events for her clients in places like New York, Atlanta, British Columbia, and many more. I will always love her for her trust in Carousel.

Lesson learned in Atlanta: It has less hotel space than Chicago, so book early. We didn't follow this advice for one show and had to find a hotel about nine miles outside Atlanta.

Paris, France–
Honolulu, Hawaii

S teven and I were about begin a vacation in Honolulu,
staying at the Kahala Hilton Hotel, which later became
the Mandarin Oriental. After a few years, the named
changed back to the Kahala. We always enjoyed our stay
because the same guests were there and we were quick to
make friends as well as meet interesting people.

Just before we were going to leave for Hawaii, I received
a call from the gentleman in charge of publicity for Trans
World Air Lines. He explained that he had a meeting planner
who was taking a group of VIPs to Paris to attend the Paris
Air Show. He wanted me to call her and see if Carousel
could help her in any way. We still had about a week to spare
before our trip to Hawaii so if we could offer some advice,
why not? Plus Tom from TWA was a nice guy.

I made the call to the meeting planner, and she explained
that she had very nice caterers from Paris she had worked
with before; they served wonderful food and had a gracious
staff. But the caterers could not understand or would not

understand that her clients wanted something different for this show than they had in the past.

She told me that her clients, a group of aircraft personnel, loved attending the Paris Air Show but wanted foods more identifiable to American cuisine. A croque monsieur (a baked ham and cheese sandwich) was okay, but her clients would also like a good old-fashioned Reuben sandwich (a corned beef, sauerkraut, and Swiss cheese with Russian dressing) as well as freshly fruit cut, not whole, and so on.

I was asked to go to Paris with her and offer some suggestions to the caterers. So Steven and I decided we would choose Paris over Hawaii, especially since airfare and lodging were provided by her client.

I have heard before that the French could be a little difficult about discussing everyday things with Americans, but food was even more sacrosanct as the French created some of the best food ever.

It was about two weeks before the upcoming Paris Air Show when the three us met with the caterers that the client felt so confident with, and I must say they were delightful. And they appreciated Steven's ability to speak a little of their language, so all worked out to everyone's satisfaction, and Carousel learned some things about how they worked.

The couple who were the owners took us all to a nice restaurant that they frequented. We ate a terrific meal and drank some good wine; I told a couple of my favorite stories about catering, and we all parted in good spirits.

We had another week booked in Paris, but the weather was awful and I wanted to stroll down the Champs-Elysees or go to dinner at a restaurant on the Left Bank. But the rain kept us in the hotel room or the dining room, so I suggested to Steven that he find us another place where it was warm and sunny. I was thinking, due to the fact that we were already in Paris, maybe Nice or San Tropez, but I did not discuss this with Steven. After a couple of hours, he came into our bedroom at the hotel to announce that we were leaving first thing in the morning, and I would be happy to know that we would once again be at Kahala in Hawaii.

Steven was quite a bit younger than me and I could see he felt really good about taking on the responsibility of making the arrangements for us to enjoy the rest of our vacation. However, I wanted to jump out the window as I remembered that we would be traveling through thirteen times zones from Paris to New York, LA, and finally Hawaii. But I said nothing.

When we finally arrived and checked into the Kahala, I was exhausted, and so was Steven; we were in bed for two days. On the third day, Steven was feeling well enough to go down to the beach and enjoy the day. I waited a while and was hungry for something other than room service, so I went down to the breakfast restaurant. But on the way, I decided to do something nice for myself. As I passed by the hotel nail salon, I thought, *Manicure.*

As I entered the salon, I was met by a lady who I guessed was the manager, telling me I would have to come back.

Yet the place was empty so I refused, and after a little conversation, I heard a voice saying it would be fine and to let the gentleman enter. Feeling rather good about myself (another time when I was impressed by my self-importance), I entered and noticed a little middle-aged Japanese lady getting a manicure and pedicure. She seemed to be getting a lot of attention. I figured she must be the owner of this salon. The lady manicurist sat me down and nervously started on my manicure.

As I sat quietly getting this manicure, I noticed the owner getting a pedicure and figured it would be a nice gesture to get a pedicure as well.

I looked in her direction, and as soon as our eyes met, I asked her how she was enjoying the pedicure. She smiled and replied that it was very relaxing and that I should have one as well. It seemed like in no time we were in a long conversation. She asked me where I was from, what I did for a living, my family, and much more.

I knew she was Japanese and owned the shop, but I didn't need to know anything else. I thought she was a potential client and it would be good business to engage her in conversation. Except during those moments of quiet time, I did wonder about her and this empty nail salon, thinking, *If it were mine, I would have a heart attack seeing no one but the both of us in here.* But that was not my problem, so as soon as I was finished, I simply said a gentlemanly goodbye and left.

Steven and I met for lunch. He noticed how nice my nails looked, was pleased, and I told him of my experience in the nail salon.

After maybe three days had passed, we were at the pool and decided to go up to our room to take a nap and get ready for dinner. As we approached the elevators, there was a large crowd blocking the entrance, so as I sometimes do, I tried to squeeze my way to the front. A very large man said to me, "Excuse me, sir, would you mind waiting for a few minutes?" And I of course objected, saying that I was a guest there, and we just wanted to go to our room.

Suddenly, a lady's voice said, "Is that you, Bill? Please join us." The crowd opened up, and there she was: the owner of the nail salon. The elevators doors opened, and about six or eight of us got in. I noticed Steven was as stiff as a rock, but I pushed our floor and bid the lady goodbye once again.

When Steven and I were alone in the hallway to our room, I told him that was the owner of the nail salon that I had told him about. He put his hand over his face and said that I should start reading newspapers.

As we entered our room, he showed me the paper, and on the cover was Empress Masako, the wife of Emperor Naruhito of Japan.

The Oscars

B ecause we were catering so many movie premieres, we always kept copies of the *Hollywood Reporter* and *Variety*, both show business papers, and read what was projected for an upcoming premiere, a possible cast party, or maybe even a star's wedding. In fact, we did the wedding of actress Cindy Williams of *Laverne & Shirley* to actor Bill Hudson.

Well anyway, after reading those magazines and watching the Academy Awards one year, I would hear actors during their acceptance speeches express their thanks, but all seemed to emphasize the long hours and hard work of moviemaking, which got me going. Long hours and hard work! No one works longer or harder on these premieres than the servers, bartenders, and captains, and of course, they are never recognized.

So I wrote a letter to Army Archer, telling him of my dismay with the Academy, all along thinking that the best I could hope for would be to maybe to get the name Carousel Catering in print.

A few weeks later, Army told of my letter and stated that he had attended events that we catered and was sure that our service deserved at least an award for "valor." He would pass on this letter to those in charge.

Dream

I dreamed that I was sitting in a restaurant alone somewhere; it looked like San Diego. It was night, and I was having dinner when for some reason I happened to look up, and there he was, standing by the "Wait to Be Seated" sign: Steven, smiling as he always did. I was a little scared, but before I knew it, I got up and ran to him. We hugged for what seemed like hours, and then I bombarded him with questions. He just continued to smile at me, and his eyes showed he still cared. Then he said, "Stay focused on your new project." He said it twice, and as always, I was not really listening. All I wanted to do was to go home with him again.

Then I woke up and realized there in our bed was Axel, my current partner. It had been twenty-one years since Steven had passed, and Axel said I was yelling in my sleep all night.

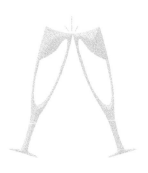

My Ride Has Come to an End

ifty years have gone by since my Carousel Catering story began. Looking back on those wonderful adventures and events, some of which are detailed in this book, I realize what a terrific life was laid out for me.

Approaching my eighty-first year, I am sad to admit that my body and mind aren't as sharp as they once were. However, it has been said that when one door closes, another opens—usually for your greater good. A very nice gentleman named Harold Matzner, owner of a five-star restaurant and executive catering operation, as well as a generous entrepreneur, believed that Carousel should remain as is and offered to purchase the company. I accepted, and everybody is happy, so I took the next step. Hence, this book.

In the beginning of this book, I quoted Henry David Thoreau.

If one advances confidently in the direction
of his dreams, and endeavors to live the life

which he has imagined, he will meet with a success unexpected in common hours.

If only one person reads this book and is inspired to walk confidently in the direction of his or her dreams, believing, *If this author can, so can I,* then I will have accomplished my goal.

MENUS

Elizabeth Taylor Passion for Women Menu

Tray-Passed Hors d'Oeuvres

Shrimp Lollipops
Served with sweet and pungent sauce.

Southwest Crab Cakes
Dungeness crab with onion, celery, fresh herbs, and diced red, green, and jalapeño peppers.

Parmesan and Shallot Soufflé
Sautéed shallots with parmesan and romano cheeses piped onto toasted bread rounds and broiled golden.

Slow-Roasted Red and Yellow Tomatoes
With chopped basil and Boursin served on grilled slices of herbed rustic bread.

Salad Course

Salad Caprice
Sliced red and yellow tomatoes with high-moisture mozzarella accented with red and yellow beet stars and heirloom cherry tomatoes finished with borage flower, basil, and pesto champagne vinaigrette.

Entrée Course

Parmesan-Crusted Chilean Sea Bass with Lemon-Sage Sauce

Encrusted with parsley, lemon zest, panko bread crumbs, and parmesan sautéed in butter and olive oil and finished with a sage-and-lemon wine sauce.

Rack of Lamb Shikar Style

Baby lamb chops marinated in soy, cardamom, curry, ginger, and garlic, slowly roasted over mesquite coals and accompanied by peach chutney.

Peeled Jumbo Asparagus

With orange-ginger baby carrots.

Angel Hair Flan

Angel hair pasta baked in parmesan-scented cream custard with garlic, thyme, and nutmeg.

Cheesy Breadsticks and Grilled Flatbreads

Dessert Course

Trio of Desserts

Pots de crème, mini pecan pie, and lemon fruit tart, garnished with whipped cream and jumbo strawberry.

HERBALIFE AT HOME OF
KENNY ROGERS

Soup and Salad Course

Off-Broadway surprise soup and heirloom tomato salad.

Entrée Course

Lemon Parmesan Chicken
Served with a lemon-sage sauce.

Peeled Duo Asparagus and Orange-Ginger Glazed Carrots

Angel Hair Flan

Angel hair pasta baked in parmesan-scented cream custard with garlic, thyme, and nutmeg.

Dessert Course

Trio of Desserts
Cheesecake square, lemon fruit tart, and cranberry pecan brownie, garnished with whipped cream, raspberry sauce, and jumbo strawberry.

Dr. Pepper Maui

Tray-Passed Hors d'Oeuvres

Herb Chicken and Artichoke Salad
Served in a wonton cup with minced chicken, thyme, chives, mozzarella, and dijonnaise.

Shrimp Lollipops
Served with sweet and pungent sauce.

Chili Garlic Beef Skewers
Skewered filet of beef marinated in garlic, chilies, soy, olive and sesame oils, and grilled to perfection.

Beggar's Purse
Curried lamb wonton.

Ahi Tuna Taco
Served in a wonton taco shell with mango salsa.

Parmesan and Shallot Soufflé
Sautéed shallots with parmesan and romano cheeses piped onto toasted bread rounds and broiled until golden.

Salad Course

Duo of Salads
Mini iceberg wedge with diced tomato.
Romaine wedge with parmesan crisp, drizzled with a balsamic reduction and served with a Boursin crostini.

Entrée Course

Pan-Seared Filet of Beef
Served with an organic wild mushroom ragout.

Or

Seared Breast of Duck
Marinated in soy and sherry, served with a port wine cherry sauce.

Haricot Verts and Carrot Bundles
Accented with snipped chives.

Garlic Mashed Potatoes
Island Almond, Wheat, and Squaw Rolls
Served with crocks of butter.

Dessert Course

Trio of Desserts
Mini pecan pie, lemon meringue pie, gluten-free oatmeal scotch chipper, garnished with seasonal berries.

Tray-Passed Hors d'Oeuvres

Borneo Marinated Fish

Diced Chilean sea bass marinated in lime juice, shallots, finely shredded ginger, mirin, white balsamic, chopped coriander, and celery.

Asparagus Wrapped with Prosciutto and Puff Pastry

Flavored with dijon.

Cranberry Chicken Salad

Served on toasted carrot raisin walnut bread.

Parmesan and Shallot Soufflé

Sautéed shallots with parmesan and romano cheeses piped onto toasted bread rounds and broiled until golden.

Oven-Fired Quesadillas

Monterey Jack and cheddar cheese combined with fire-roasted chilies and Mediterranean olives, served with guacamole.

Stationed Hors d'Oeuvres and Desserts

Shrimp Lollipops

Served with a sweet and pungent sauce.

Mini Spinach and Mushroom Frittatas

Accented with goat cheese.

Seared Beef Tenderloin

Seared filet set atop a Boursin-scented crostini with parsley, capers, and mustard horseradish sauce.

Chocolate Brownie Triangles

Gluten-free oatmeal scotch chippers.

Acknowledgments

I want to thank the following:

Chip Clements, the editor of this book, for his patience, kindness, and expertise; without Chip, this book would not be complete.

David Erickson, the executive chef of Carousel, for always standing beside me when I had some crazy ideas for events and for training his staff to make Carousel always look good.

John Bowab for always listening to me and for giving me great advice on many subjects regarding this book.

And of course, Axel Pichardo for being so understanding while showing better ways to accomplish what I wanted on the computer.

I want to also thank Lois Fletcher for her patience throughout this whole experience.

Lightning Source UK Ltd.
Milton Keynes UK
UKHW011343100820
367994UK00003B/55/J